This book may be kept

MONEY AND STOCK PRICES

MONEY
and
STOCK PRICES

by BERYL W. SPRINKEL, Ph.D.

Vice President and Economist
and Director of Research
Harris Trust and Savings Bank
Chicago, Illinois

1964

RICHARD D. IRWIN, INC.
HOMEWOOD, ILLINOIS

First printing, June, 1964

Library of Congress Catalog Card No. 64–21025

PRINTED IN THE UNITED STATES OF AMERICA

To my wife, children, and parents in appreciation of their encouragement and patience.

Preface

THE PURPOSE of this book is to develop a new and practical technique for improving the art of investment timing of common stock purchases and sales. In a broader sense, the text integrates the explanation of forces determining trends in equity prices with modern monetary theory. Although investors have long recognized that a relation exists between economic trends and financial markets, no satisfactory rationale existed. Stock prices have usually moved in advance of significant changes in economic trends. Unless one is willing to attribute uncanny sagacity to investors, which the writer is unwilling to do, the facts seem to defy explanation. It is the basic thesis of this exposition that economic and stock price changes have a common "cause," changes in money, which directly influence the demand for assets such as common stocks as well as the demand for goods and services. The money or liquidity explanation is supported by most stock price and economic trends since at least World War I.

The text utilizes analytical disciplines from the areas of monetary theory, business cycles, and investments. After the basic thesis and the supporting data are developed, an analysis of the process of monetary change is presented, with emphasis upon methods of interpretation and measurement. The process of business cycle movements is reviewed and the relation of monetary change and the National Bureau of Economic Research's leading, coincident, and lagging indicators is developed and evaluated. Finally, the monetary or liquidity approach to timing common stock sales and purchases is tested and results are compared with alternative approaches. It is emphasized throughout the exposition that the monetary approach to investment and economic analysis and decision making should not be considered to be an infallible gimmick but should be viewed as another useful tool to be integrated into existing knowledge.

The ideas and methods of analysis and measurement should be of use to all investors including both professionals and the small investor managing his own funds. A serious attempt is made to avoid technical economic jargon comprehensible to only professional economists. Also, college students studying in the fields of monetary theory, business cycles, investments, and money markets will find this exposition a useful supplement to the traditional textbook.

I am grateful to many colleagues both for stimulating me to work on this project as well as for suggesting improvements. I am particularly indebted to Reuben A. Kessel, Phillip Cagan, George Wallace, Myron J. Gordon, Robert W. Johnson, William C. Norby, and Warren L. Fellingham. But most of all I am grateful for the stimuli of two of my former teachers, Professor Milton Friedman and Professor Marshall D. Ketchum of the University of Chicago. Professor Friedman taught me much about money and provided stimulus and insight into problems encountered in this study. He and Mrs. Anna J. Schwartz also graciously provided unpublished data on the money stock at an early stage of this study. Professor Ketchum initially aroused my interest in business cycles and the problem of investment timing and also provided encouragement for the study. Shirley Wilson efficiently executed most of the computations and charts. Any remaining errors are mine.

I am also appreciative of publisher and author permission to quote various published works.

BERYL W. SPRINKEL

Flossmoor, Illinois
April, 1964

Table of Contents

List of Charts

List of Tables

I

In the Beginning

THE SEARCH for a method of anticipating major movements in common stock prices is eagerly pressed forward, but success has been as elusive as the search for the Fountain of Youth. Stock price trends are particularly difficult to predict, since they appear to have no close and simple relation to the general pattern of business and profits. It is true that economic activity and stock prices go in the same direction about two-thirds of the time, but it is the other third that is most interesting and potentially most profitable. Usually, stock price changes move well ahead of subsequent business changes so that economic activity and share prices are moving in separate directions at the turning points in the market. Occasionally, stock prices forge a pattern all their own, apparently unrelated to the underlying business and profit trend. Even if predictions of future business trends were usually reliable, it would not be possible to detect turning points in stock prices unless business cycle turning points could be projected several months into the future. Unfortunately, business cycle forecasting is a hazardous art, particularly near turning points, and the longer the forecast period, the greater the probability of error.

Some market analysts have recognized the tendency of stock price changes to lead business cycle turning points, and have argued that the explanation for this relationship lies in the sagacity of the few analysts who foresaw the subsequent business change and achieved the appropriate action in the market prior to the change. Stock price and business data are usually consistent with such an interpretation, but this hypothesis provides no guide to less farsighted observers. Furthermore, this explanation is not subject to test, for even though we may not know of anyone who consistently took the proper market action prior to subsequent economic changes, such a person or group of persons well may exist. To complicate matters further, it is difficult to segregate fact from fancy. It always appears easier to locate investors who by their own testimony made the proper investment decision prior to a *past* market change than it is to find investors who announce their investment moves prior to predicted market movements which subsequently occur. The leading stock price-business cycle relation has existed as far back into history as data are available; therefore, if someone knew the secret in the past, it was handed on to his successors. But the leading relation has been so stable over such a long period of time that we can be reasonably certain something of more basic economic significance than a few successful forecasters explains the consistency.

Although economists have long been concerned with attempting to explain changes in general economic activity, relative prices of competing goods and services, and changes in the general price level, very little attention has been given to explaining broad price changes in assets such as common stocks. In fact, most economists contend changes in stock prices are not amenable to economic analysis. It is apparently believed equity prices are determined more by chance than by reason. The oldest theory, and the most valid, as will be argued subsequently, purporting to explain changes in aggregate monetary demand relies on changes in liquidity or the stock of money as the independent or causal factor. This theory is generally called the quantity theory of money.

If in fact changes in the stock of money or liquidity influence the willingness of consumers and investors to exchange money for goods and assets, there should be a demonstrable relation between monetary change on the one hand and business and stock price changes on the other. Chart 1 relates peaks and troughs in the rate of change in the stock of money—demand deposits of commercial banks plus currency—to changes in stock prices and the underlying business trend. It is readily apparent that contracting liquidity usually precedes both declining stock prices and sagging business activity. The average time span between declining liquidity and weak stock prices has been about fifteen months, whereas weaker liquidity has preceded a business contraction twenty months on average. Therefore, stock prices have usually declined an average of about five months prior to a weaker business trend.

In the past 45 years, however, there have been two sizable market breaks that were not preceded by contracting liquidity or shortly followed by a business decline. These breaks occurred in 1939–40 and, recently, in 1962. Factors unfavorable to stock ownership more than offset existing economic and liquidity forces. The beginning and spreading of World War II undoubtedly destroyed confidence in stock prices in 1939 and 1940 despite the underlying favorable liquidity and business trend. Business and liquidity trends in 1962 were also favorable, but other unfavorable factors dominated. It is possible to fabricate an ad hoc explanation of the 1962 break, but it cannot be tested over a series of market breaks, since it is unique to the 1962 episode. An explanation might consist of such factors as: (1) weak technical market condition due to excessive speculation, particularly in new issues; (2) loss of confidence in the administration after executive interference with steel price determination; (3) unusually high price-earnings on common stocks; (4) the sharp increase to a 4 per cent rate of return on savings deposits in commercial banks. Little confidence can be placed in the above explanation, since it cannot be adequately tested. In any event, liquidity changes did not portend either the 1939–40 or the 1962 market break. The market, however, recovered lost ground and rose to new highs in both cases before liquidity turned unfavorable. Changing liquidity trends are, therefore, not always the dominant force affecting stock prices, even though they usually are.

Chart 1 also clearly indicates that rising liquidity trends precede a recovery in stock prices and an expansion in economic activity. But the elapsed lead time is less. Expanding liquidity typically precedes a rise in stock prices by about two months, whereas it precedes an expanding business trend by about eight months. There appears to have been no significant exception to this leading relation in the past 45 years.

It therefore follows that an investor who based his stock market decisions over the past 45 years upon expanding and contracting liquidity would have participated in all bull markets and would have avoided all but two bear markets. Following the two misses, the market eventually recouped losses and reached new highs prior to the next bear indication. Investors searching for and realistically hoping to find the magic touchstone which will bring certainty in all future stock market timing decisions should cease reading at this point. Those wishing to improve the probability of being right on future investment timing decisions may find this book of interest.

If an investor can properly measure and interpret changing liquidity trends, the proper investment action is usually indicated in advance of the time for action. Therefore, an investor can develop an additional safeguard against the hazard to which many investors are prone—buying at high markets when optimism is at a peak and selling at the low when pessimism is rampant. But before a new investment technique can be used successfully, it must be understood. Understanding is the first hesitant but necessary step toward developing confidence. Without confidence, the temptation to abandon an investment ap-

CHART 1
LIQUIDITY CHANGE AND STOCK PRICES

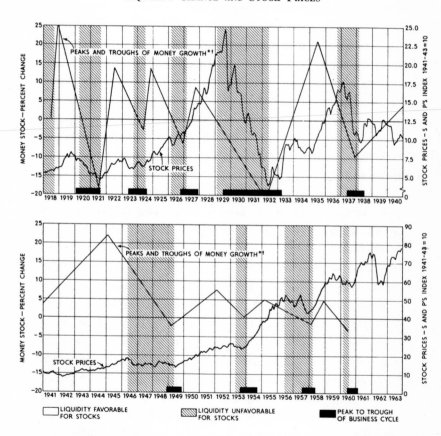

Source: Standard & Poor's 425 Stock Industrial Index, National Bureau of Economic Research, Inc., Federal Reserve Board.
   °Demand deposits adjusted + currency (seasonally adjusted).
   †Annual rate of monthly change, 6-month moving average.
   Price index scale different on upper and lower charts.
   Peaks and troughs of postwar money growth are based on money stock series available prior to modest revisions published in the August, 1962, *Federal Reserve Bulletin.*
   Data presented in Appendix B.

proach when doubts first arise is irresistible. It is of course, much easier to state the above principle than to follow it in practice.

The remainder of this book will deal with such questions as the following. What is money and liquidity? Why should liquidity change influence economic activity and equity prices? What determines changes in liquidity trends? How do the Federal Reserve and commercial banking systems fit into this picture? How can liquidity change best be measured? What are other useful approaches to business cycle prediction? Why is liquidity change a major causal factor in business cycles? What are the hazards of applying liquidity analysis to the timing of stock market action? What investment returns would have resulted from applying the liquidity approach in the past? What effect should tax factors have on investment timing decisions? These questions are not exhaustive but are meant to be suggestive of the discussion to follow. Now let us briefly consider the sixty-four-dollar question: Why should liquidity or monetary changes make a difference?

II

The Explanation

in a Nutshell

WHY THEORY?

IT IS an easy task for an imaginative analyst to "explain" past business and stock price trends by resort to ad hoc reasoning. Unfortunately, there are frequently as many explanations as there are imaginative analysts. Clearly, the objective of a careful student of economic affairs should be to isolate a simple and ubiquitous explanation which is consistent with factual trends over a long period of time and in widely varying circumstances. To fabricate a tailor-made explanation for each event may create the impression of ingenuity or freshness of approach but provide little enlightenment on future events. Many observers apparently feel that to be satisfactory an explanation must be highly descriptive of the event under analysis. This approach dotes on citing many variables and their possible influence. This eclectic approach gives the impression of being exhaustive, but because of the limitations of both the human mind and mathematical formulations, the results are frequently of limited use.

The approach taken in subsequent analysis may well appear limited in scope and narrow in concept. But it will attempt to isolate a major variable which offers a plausible explanation consistent with most observed empirical patterns of equity prices and business cycle trends. The viewpoint taken is that the usefulness of a theory is not measured by its ability to describe but by its ability to predict. A theory which does not describe in detail the results under question may in one sense be labeled unrealistic, but may at the same time be extremely useful if it is capable of predicting many later events. In other words, a theory may be properly rejected if it is incapable of yielding useful predictions but cannot be disproven by questioning the "reasonableness" of underlying assumptions. A theory capable of yielding useful predictions concerning economic events must concentrate on the most basic underlying relations, and will, therefore, be as simple as possible and narrow in scope but broad in terms of useful implications.

WHAT IS MONEY?

Money is easily the most sought after, the most frequently condemned, and the least understood element in our complex world. Confusion over the concept of money is partly due to lack of agreement on definition of the term. To the poor man pursuing money so that he may buy the basic necessities of life, it may represent the only means of survival in a cold, competitive world. To others more fortunate, money may represent the means of acquiring the material and spiritual extras in life that make living easier and more rewarding. To the miser, money may not represent a means to an end, but rather an end in itself. To the social philosopher who does not approve of letting the free market determine how money is spent, it may be roundly condemned because it stands as a symbol of greed and inequity.

Since some form of money or credit is used in the production, sale, and exchange of all goods and services, it is clear that money is a pervasive phenomenon in our free, competitive economy. Because of its widespread use and pervasive influence, it is not difficult to imagine that money can be a force for great good or evil in the economy as a whole. A proper understanding of its effect on the economy can be used for both public and personal gain. Specifically, a proper understanding of the role and influence of money can contribute greatly to our understanding of changes in the business cycle and the financial markets. Although it would be irresponsible to contend that such an understanding makes possible perfect predictions of business and market changes, monetary analysis can provide useful guidance. Imperfect though our understanding may be, enough is known now about the role of money and its effects on economic activity in general and the financial markets in particular to enable an astute investor to profitably take these factors into consideration.

To the economist when considering it from an analytical viewpoint, money represents a medium by which goods and services can be exchanged conveniently, and because of its widespread acceptance in trade, it frequently acts as a liquid medium for storing value as do other forms of assets. Money performs so many roles in our economy, some of which are performed by all assets, that it is impossible to specify uniquely on mere a priori grounds what the term covers. Clearly, cash in circulation (representing liabilities of the U.S. Treasury and the Federal Reserve banks) is money. Demand deposits in banks also are money, since they are readily acceptable in most circumstances, even though it may be difficult to write a check against a demand deposit when you have no satisfactory means of identification. Certainly, time deposits in commercial banks partially serve the liquidity role of money as do shares in savings and loan associations, deposits in mutual savings banks,

U.S. government savings bonds, and short-term U.S. government securities. To a lesser extent, other less liquid assets such as long-term bonds, stocks, and real estate act as a store of value. There is, clearly, a continuum of assets which more or less meets the store-of-liquidity specification for money, even though such assets do not serve as a medium of exchange. It is, therefore, impossible to select a nonarbitrary definition of money based on a priori grounds alone.

The selection of a meaningful definition of money must be based on empirical evidence rather than theoretical arguments, since the last approach does not yield a clear-cut answer. The definition selected should be the one which bears the most consistent relationship to subsequent economic events.

Three recent studies have investigated the relation of money to the economy, and each attempted to determine the "proper" definition of money by use of empirical evidence.[1]

Meltzer and Feige concluded money should be defined to include only demand deposits and currency. The Friedman-Meiselman study concluded that time deposits of commercial banks should be added, since their money-income correlations were improved moderately. Each study rejected the inclusion of still broader assets such as savings and loan shares.

When the word money is used later in this text, it will refer simply to the total of the public's holdings of coin, currency, and demand deposits in banks. Money will, therefore, consist of private demand deposits subject to check and cash. The only defensible reasons for thus arbitrarily restricting our definitions are that the concept is simple and money so defined is

---

[1] Milton Friedman and David Meiselman, "The Relative Stability of Monetary Velocity and the Investment Multiplier in the United States, 1897–1958," *Stabilization Policies*, prepared for the Commission on Money and Credit (Englewood Cliffs, N.J.: Prentice-Hall, 1963), pp. 165–268; Allan H. Meltzer, "The Demand for Money: The Evidence From the Time Series," *Journal of Political Economy*. June, 1963, pp. 219–46; Edgar L. Feige, "The Demand for Liquid Assets; A Temporal Cross-Section Analysis" (Ph.D. thesis, University of Chicago, 1963).

apparently as closely related to subsequent economic events as would be money more broadly defined.

HOW DOES MONEY INFLUENCE THE ECONOMY AND STOCK PRICES?

The impulse of changing money influences the economy and asset prices through its impact on total demands for goods, services and assets. Potential for economic production is determined by real supply factors such as the size and quality of the labor force, average hours of work, the stock and quality of capital, the state of technology, and the efficiency with which resources are combined. The degree of utilization of economic resources is determined primarily by the volume of total demand—that is, whether or not demand is large enough to utilize available resources at existing prices. In other words, the actual production of goods and services will depend not only on real supply factors but also on changes in total demands. In given supply conditions, the volume of total demand will determine the amount of actual production, income, and employment attained in the economy. But how does changing money influence aggregate demand?

Although the amount of money actually circulating in the economy is largely beyond the control of private spending units, the demand for money will vary with such factors as real income and interest rates. The higher the levels of income, the larger the amount of money spending units desire to hold. Also, the lower the level of interest rates, the greater the amount of money spending units would be willing to hold, since the cost of maintaining liquidity is reduced. Individuals and business firms will attempt to distribute their holdings of assets in such a way that the income or satisfaction from like units will yield the same benefits. If individuals and businesses feel they have inadequate liquidity, they will attempt to convert non-liquid assets into liquid funds. Also, by reducing expenditures relative to incomes, individual spending units will attempt to build up their liquidity. But these actions will tend to place downward price pressure on less liquid assets such as common stocks. The attempt to reduce spending relative to income will have the effect of reducing total demands and, hence, reduce incomes, employment, and, eventually, the general price level. Therefore, reduced liquidity resulting from reduced monetary expansion or monetary contraction contains the forces to prevent further increases in total demand and, hence, increases in real economic activity.

Conversely, a rapid increase in overall liquidity resulting from an increase in monetary growth would tend to have the opposite effect. As "excessive" liquidity developed, spending units would be induced to exchange money for less liquid forms of assets. This action would tend to place upward pressure on the price of less liquid assets such as common stocks. Also, spending units would be inclined to attempt to reduce liquidity by increasing spending on goods and services relative to the current flow of income. This action would raise the overall level of monetary demand, and would result in a higher level of production of goods and services if unemployed resources were available or would place upward pressure on the general price level if full employment of resources obtained.

Now to briefly recapitulate the argument. It was demonstrated that changing monetary growth typically precedes changing equity prices which, in turn, usually move in advance of overall business fluctuations. Liquidity change, as defined, consists of changes in money—that is, demand deposits of commercial banks and currency. A condensed version of a long lived and recently revived theory, generally labeled the quantity theory of money, was presented to show that this explanation is consistent with observed trends in money, stock prices, and business cycles. Although this explanation may at first blush appear unrealistic in a descriptive sense, readers are cautioned not to reject the point of view unless it yields inadequate predictions. The next major step is to understand the forces which cause a change in the stock of money and, hence, trigger the chain of responses in the equity market and total economic activity. Unless the major causal forces can be isolated, a developing liquidity trend cannot be understood, nor can a prospective change be detected.

III

What Determines Trends
in the Stock of Money?

THE SIMPLE and essentially correct answer to the question posed above is that monetary policy as formulated and executed by the Federal Reserve System establishes the prevailing trend in the stock of money. But adequate comprehension of the answer must be based on knowledge of the elementary structure of the banking systems, an understanding of the process of money creation and destruction, and the ability to analyze changes in the sources and uses of commercial bank reserve funds. Although mastery of these matters is inevitably somewhat tedious, the results will hopefully be worth the effort.

BASIC STRUCTURE OF THE BANKING SYSTEM

Approximately 45 per cent of the nation's 13,400 commercial banks are members of the Federal Reserve System. But these member banks are the larger institutions and, hence, account for about 85 per cent of total demand deposits which is the major component of the money stock. The Federal Reserve

System is thus able to determine changes in the stock of money because of its ability to regulate banks which contain all demand deposits.

Member banks of the Federal Reserve System assume certain obligations in return for receiving privileges of membership.[1] The primary obligation so far as monetary change is concerned is that of maintaining legal reserves on deposit without interest at the Reserve bank (except those reserves held as vault cash). Other subsidiary requirements include: (1) the remittance at par for checks drawn against them when presented by a Reserve bank for payment; (2) compliance with various federal laws, regulations, and conditions of membership concerning the adequacy of capital, mergers with other banks, establishment of branches, relations with holding companies, interlocking directorates, and loan and investment limitations.

From the point of view of monetary control, the most important privileges extended member banks are the following: (1) the privilege of borrowing from the Reserve bank, subject to criteria for discounting set by statute and regulation, when a temporary need for funds arises; (2) the privilege of using Federal Reserve facilities for collecting checks, settling clearing balances, and transferring funds to other locations. Subsidiary privileges include: (1) obtaining currency from the Reserve bank when required; (2) sharing in the informational facilities provided by the System; (3) participation in the election of six of the nine directors of the Federal Reserve bank for their district; (4) receiving a divident of 6 per cent on the paid-in capital stock of the Federal Reserve bank which each member bank is required to purchase as a condition of membership.

There are 12 Federal Reserve districts across the nation, and

---

[1] For greater detail see: Board of Governors of the Federal Reserve System, *The Federal Reserve System, Purposes and Functions,* 1961.

a Federal Reserve bank is located in each district. Several of the Federal Reserve banks also have branches. While the Federal Reserve banks earn an income, largely from the U.S. government securities owned, their operations are not carried on primarily for profit but for the purpose of conducting monetary policy. Income is used for paying expenses and maintaining a proper surplus. The remainder of the earnings is paid to the U.S. Treasury.

The top policy-making body of the Central Bank is the Board of Governors of the Federal Reserve System with offices in Washington, D.C. It consists of seven members appointed by the President of the United States and subject to confirmation by the Senate. Board appointments are for terms of 14 years, with terms expiring every two years. The Board's main functions are to formulate and execute monetary policy and supervise the operations of the Federal Reserve System. It has full authority over changes in reserve requirements, and also "reviews and determines" discount or borrowing rates established by each of the 12 Federal Reserve banks.

The Federal Open Market Committee has responsibility for changes made in the System's portfolio of government securities. It decides the amount and timing of purchases and sales of government securities in the open market. The authority to buy and sell government securities is one of the most important monetary controls exercised by the Federal Reserve System. Membership on the Open Market Committee comprises of the seven members of the Board of Governors and five of the twelve presidents of district Federal Reserve banks. Actual purchases and sales of securities for the Federal Open Market Committee are made through the facilities of the Federal Reserve Bank of New York.[2]

---

[2] For detail on the New York money market and open market operations see: Carl H. Madden, *The Money Side of "The Street"* (Federal Reserve Bank of New York, 1960).

The Federal Reserve System also has a reserve requirement which states that Federal Reserve banks must hold gold certificates as reserves amounting to a stipulated proportion of their liabilities in the form of Federal Reserve notes and deposits. In the U.S. monetary system, the U.S. Treasury is custodian of all monetary reserves held in the form of gold. Reserves of the Federal Reserve banks therefore take the form of certificates which represent the actual gold. The legal gold ratio for Federal Reserve banks is now 25 per cent for each category of liabilities. The Board of Governors has the authority to suspend temporarily the reserve requirements of the Reserve banks.

The Federal Reserve System therefore exercises control over the nation's commercial banking system through its influence on member banks which hold about 85 per cent of total demand deposits, the major component of the money stock. Member banks must hold the bulk of their reserves with the district Federal Reserve bank. The Federal Reserve System influences the amount and cost of acquiring bank reserves by use of three major tools: (1) changes in reserve requirements, (2) changes in the discount rate, and (3) open market operations. The Board of Governors has complete authority in determining reserve requirements; discount rates are established by each of the 12 Federal Reserve banks, and the Board of Governors "reviews and determines" the rates; and finally the Federal Open Market Committee consisting of the seven board members and five of the twelve regional Federal Reserve bank presidents determines purchases and sales in the open market from the System's portfolio of government securities. So long as the gold reserve requirement is in effect, the maximum amount of Federal Reserve liabilities in the form of notes and deposits is set by the amount of gold certificates held. With a requirement of 25 per cent, total Reserve bank liabilities in the form of notes and deposits may not exceed four times the amount of gold certificates held.

Money is an asset of its holder, but it is a liability of some financial institutions. The various components of the stock of money, consisting of demand deposits and currency, is a liability of either commercial banks, the U.S. Treasury or Federal Reserve banks. All demand deposits included in the money stock are liabilities of commercial banks; Treasury notes and silver certificates are liabilities of the U.S. Treasury, and finally, Federal Reserve notes are liabilities of the Federal Reserve banks. Therefore, it is apparent that the stock of money can vary only as the liabilities of various financial institutions change.

In developing an understanding of the U.S. banking system and the process of monetary change, it is useful to observe partial balance sheets or T-accounts of three institutions—the U.S. Treasury, the Federal Reserve System and the commercial banking system. We are interested in only those portions of total assets and liabilities closely related to the monetary system.

TABLE 1
PARTIAL BALANCE SHEETS, DECEMBER 31, 1962
(Billions of Dollars)

U.S. Treasury

Gold	$16.0	Gold certificates	$15.7
Deposits with Federal		Treasury currency	
Reserve banks	.6	outstanding	5.6

Federal Reserve System

Gold certificates	$15.7	Federal Reserve notes	30.2
		Deposits of	
		member banks	17.5
		U.S. Treasury	
		deposits	.6
		Foreign deposits	.2
		Other deposits	.4

Commercial Banking System

Deposits with Federal Reserve	17.5	Demand deposits adjusted	121.7
		Time deposits adjusted	96.7

Holders of Money

Currency in circulation	$ 30.7	
Demand deposits adjusted	121.7	

First let us consider the U.S. Treasury which is the custodian of the monetary gold stock. Most changes in the country's gold stock are the result of transactions with foreign countries. On December 31, 1962, the U.S. gold stock amounted to $16.0 billion, as indicated in Table 1, and gold certificates had been issued to Federal Reserve banks amounting to $15.7 billion. Gold is an asset of the Treasury, and gold certificates are a non-interest-bearing liability. Also, Treasury deposits with Federal Reserve banks appears as an asset. In addition, $5.6 billion of Treasury currency, which is part of the stock of money, had been issued by the Treasury and was, therefore, another non-interest-bearing liability.

The Federal Reserve System holds all the gold certificates issued by the Treasury, so this item appears in the Federal Reserve partial balance sheet as an asset. Since Federal Reserve banks have a statutory reserve requirement in the form of gold certificates amounting to 25 per cent of their liabilities in the form of deposits and notes, the $15.7 billion of gold certificates established a ceiling of $62.8 billion for deposits and notes. Total Federal Reserve liabilities subject to reserve requirements on December 31, 1962, amounted to $48.9 billion consisting largely of $30.2 billion Federal Reserve notes, which are a part of the money stock, and $17.5 billion of member bank deposits which serve as member bank reserves. Most U.S. Treasury payments are made by checks written on a Federal Reserve bank, so U.S. Treasury funds are on deposit with Federal Reserve banks. The required reserves of the Federal Reserve banks were equal to 25 per cent of $48.9 billion, or $12.2 billion. Therefore, excess reserves of the Federal Reserve System in the form of gold certificates amounted to $3.5 billion; that is, the difference between total reserves and required reserves was $3.5 billion. A measure of the excess reserve ratio can be made by computing the actual reserve ratio (gold certificate reserves ÷ deposits + Federal Reserve notes) and comparing it with the required reserve ratio of 25 per cent. It is, therefore, apparent that the actual reserve ratio was 32 per cent ($15.7 ÷ $48.9), so that the excess reserve ratio was 7 per cent.

The relevant portion of the commercial banking system's balance sheet consists of the asset representing deposits with the Federal Reserve banks which serve as the commercial banking system's reserves, and liabilities consisting of deposits. The reserve requirement ratio for commercial banks demand deposits amounted to 12 per cent for country banks and 16.5 per cent for reserve city commercial banks. The weighted average demand deposit-required reserve ratio is now about 15 per cent. All commercial banks are required to keep a 4 per cent reserve against time deposits. On December 26, 1962, excess reserves of the commercial banking system amounted to $561 million—that is, the difference between total reserves and required reserves.

Finally, the stock of money consisting of currency outstanding and demand deposits is at all times held by some owner and, therefore, appears as an asset in the combined partial balance sheet of money holders.

THE PROCESS OF MONETARY CHANGE

Since demand deposits of commercial banks are the largest and most readily controlled component of the stock of money, it is imperative that students of money understand how demand deposits change if they are to understand the process of money creation and destruction.[3] For the moment, we will suspend consideration of *how* total reserves change and concentrate on the response of the commercial banking system to a change in total reserves. As a useful first approximation, it may be stated the maximum amount of demand deposits that can be outstand-

---

[3] See Federal Reserve Bank of Chicago, *Modern Money Mechanics*, May, 1961, for a more elaborate treatment of this subject.

ing at any time is fixed by the average required reserve ratio and total reserves held by commercial banks. Commercial banks are required to maintain reserves in the form of either deposits with Federal Reserve banks or cash in their vaults of not less than a specified fraction of commercial bank deposits. Therefore, commercial bank deposits cannot exceed the amount their total reserves will support.

For example, if we assume the average required reserve ratio is 15 per cent and total reserves (available to support demand deposits) $16 billion, total demand deposits could not exceed $106.67 billion. In other words, each $1.00 of reserves could support $6.67 of demand deposits. An amount of demand deposits in excess of $106.67 billion would create a reserve deficiency which would require either an increase in reserves or a reduction in demand deposits.

But banks may maintain what are called excess reserves—in excess of the required minimum—and deposits may, therefore, be less than the amount supportable by total reserves. However, since banks enjoy no return on excess reserves—that is, the Federal Reserve pays no interest on commercial bank deposits—the profit motive insures that *most* excess funds will be loaned or invested except in very unusual circumstances such as those during the Great Depression. However, institutional and economic factors result in some excess reserves even in more normal periods. For example, excess reserves averaged $572 million or 2.8 per cent of total reserves in 1962. Most reserves will be fully utilized, since banks have an incentive to convert excess reserves to required reserves by expanding loans and/or investments and, hence, deposits. With a fixed required reserve ratio, factors that change total bank reserves will also tend to change the total stock of money in the same direction but by a multiple amount.

But what is the process by which a given increase in total reserves results in a multiple expansion in demand deposits?

An example would perhaps clear up the matter. Let us again assume an average required reserve ratio of 15 per cent for all member banks, and let us further assume that the Federal Reserve System increases total reserves by an amount of $1 million which ends up as reserves of commercial bank A.

Assume, also, that the initial increase in total reserves was brought about in a way that did not affect required reserves in the first instance. Therefore, excess reserves of commercial bank A rose $1 million also, since total reserves — required reserves = excess reserves. We will not now inquire into the means by which the Federal Reserve increased total and excess reserves but will concentrate on the effect this action might have on commercial banks.

Since commercial bank A now has excess reserves on which no return is being earned, there is an incentive to either loan or invest the funds. The effect on the stock of money would be the same regardless of whether the funds were loaned or invested. If business activity is strong, the funds would probably be loaned, since the rate of return tends to be higher, and a bank usually feels a strong responsibility to meet the credit demands of its customers. In making a loan, a bank typically accepts a promissory note in exchange for credit to the borrower's deposit account. Hence, bank A's loans (assets) and deposits (liabilities) both rise by $1 million. Total reserves are unaffected by the above transaction, but excess reserves decline by $150,000, since demand deposits, against which a 15 per cent required reserve ratio obtains, rose by $1 million. Excess reserves are now $850,000. Up to the present, the increase in the stock of money (demand deposits in this case) has been $1 million, the same as the initial increase in total reserves and excess reserves. But 85 per cent of the excess reserves remain in the banking system.

Bank A did not expect to retain the deposits created through its loan operations. Borrowers acquired the funds for spending, and checks will be drawn against the new funds and deposited in other banks. Although banks typically require compensating balances be maintained in the lending bank, this complication will be ignored, for it does not affect the essential nature of the multiple expansion process. When the funds are transferred to another bank, they are not extinguished but remain in the banking system. Whichever bank receives the new deposits will also hold an equal amount of reserves of which all but 15 per cent will be excess, that is, $850,000. We will assume that bank B which received the deposit also wants to get its excess funds to work earning a return and that the amount of the excess reserves, $850,000, is loaned to a customer. Bank B will accept a promissory note equal to $850,000 and will in return credit the borrower's deposit account for a like amount. Bank B will now have $1 million reserves more than prior to the deposit from bank A—$1.85 million deposits more than previously— and still have excess reserve amounting to $850,000 × 85 per cent, or $722,000. Bank A at this point will have lost the initial reserve and deposit, but loans would be $1 million higher. It is important to recognize that $722,000 excess reserve still remains in the banking system, even though total deposits are already increased $1.85 million on the basis of the initial increase of $1 million in total and excess reserves.

Let us trace these transactions through bank A and bank B with the aid of partial balance sheets or T-accounts. Remember that bank A made the initial loan and deposit credit because it had $1 million excess reserves. The initial deposit made in bank B is usually termed primary deposit, whereas the deposit resulting from the loan is called a derivative deposit. Note that when bank B's derivative deposit is withdrawn, deposits and reserves each will decline by $850,000, and bank B will then have zero excess reserves, even though total reserves are $150,-000 higher than prior to the primary deposits of $1 million. If the derivative deposit is made with bank C, that bank will then have excess reserves of $722,000 and can make a loan and deposit credit of that amount. At that point, total deposits will be $2.572 million greater than initially, and $614,000 excess reserves will remain in the banking system.

TABLE 2
PARTIAL BALANCE SHEETS

Bank A

(1) Loans + $1 million	Demand deposits + $1 million
(2) Reserves − $1 million	Demand deposits − $1 million

Bank B

(3) Reserves + $1 milion	Demand deposits + $1 million
Loans + $850,000	Demand deposits + $850,000

When the remaining excess reserves of $614,000 are converted into required reserves in the manner described above, the total increase in demand deposits—that is, the money stock resulting from the initial increase of $1 million in excess reserves—will be $6,666,666.67. Therefore, it is correct to say that with a given increase in excess reserves, there will be an ultimate multiple expansion in loans and/or investments which results in a multiple demand deposit expansion. The size of the potential multiple expansion will depend on the average required reserve ratio for demand deposits. The smaller the average required reserve ratio, the larger the ultimate expansion. The multiple will be equal to the reciprocal of the average required reserve ratio—that is,

$$\text{multiple} = \frac{1}{\text{average required reserve ratio.}}$$ In the above case, the expansion factor $= 1/0.15 = 6\frac{2}{3}$. The following table summarizes the response of the commercial banking system to the initial $1 million.

It is important to recognize that it was the *banking system* and not a *single bank* that achieved a multiple demand deposit

TABLE 3
MONETARY EXPANSION PROCESS

ASSETS (IN THOUSANDS OF DOLLARS)					LIABILITIES
RESERVES					
Total		Required	Excess	LOANS AND/OR INVESTMENTS	Demand Deposits
Initial Reserves Provided	1,000	0	1,000		
Expansion—Stage 1	1,000	150	850	1,000	1,000
2	1,000	278	722	1,850	1,850
3	1,000	386	614	2,572	2,572
4	1,000	478	522	3,186	3,186
5	1,000	556	444	3,708	3,708
6	1,000	623	377	4,152	4,152
7	1,000	680	320	4,529	4,529
8	1,000	728	272	4,849	4,849
9	1,000	769	231	5,121	5,121
10	1,000	803	197	5,352	5,352
Final Stage	1,000	1,000	0	6,667	6,667

expansion on the basis of a given amount of excess reserves. A single bank could make loans and/or investments equal only to the amount of excess reserves, and, hence, derivative demand deposits could rise only by a like amount. Reference to Table 2 will clarify this distinction. Bank A which began the process with $1 million excess reserves made a loan of only $1 million and credited demand deposit accounts by a like amount. At that instant, bank A still had $850,000 excess reserves which would suggest that a sizable further loan and deposit expansion was possible. Yet, if additional loans had been made and demand deposit accounts credited accordingly, the bank would have ended up in a deficit reserve position after the derivative deposits were transferred. It should be noted that after the initial derivative deposit of bank A was transferred, the bank no longer had excess reserves, since total reserves were decreased by $1 million consisting of a decrease of $850,000 in excess reserves and a reduction of $150,000 in required reserves as demand deposits declined by $1 million. Only if the derivative deposits were placed back in bank A would excess reserves remain after the transfer occurred. Therefore, although the banking system can achieve a multiple deposit and loan expansion, no individual bank can achieve that result. Expansion of loans and investments by an individual bank must remain in step with the system's expansion. Otherwise, a deficit reserve position develops which requires either the liquidation of loans and/or investments or the acquisition of additional reserves either by borrowing from the Federal Reserve bank or by borrowing reserves from other commercial banks.

It should also be understood that the stages of expansion do not occur simultaneously. An individual bank cannot participate in the expansion process until it acquires excess reserves resulting from a transfer of a deposit from another bank. Because some banks may continuously maintain excess reserves and other banks may utilize excess reserves only after a considerable time lag, the process may continue for some time. Moreover, expansion of deposits may never reach its theoretical limit because of the indefinite retention of excess reserves by some commercial banks. There is, in fact, a tendency for excess reserves to build up as interest rates decline, because the return from using the funds is less. This does not necessarily mean that individual banks are "wasting money," since the amount of excess reserves in an individual bank may be so small that it is not worth the expense incurred in loaning or investing the funds. The profit motive tends to keep the volume of excess reserves at a low level.

Not only does a multiple expansion process result when banks gain excess reserves, but also a multiple contraction occurs when excess reserves are removed from the banking system. Similar to the expansion process, an *individual bank* can eliminate a reserve deficiency by reducing loans and/or investments by a like amount. A $1,000 security sale by an individual bank will reduce its reserve deficiency by $1,000, but total required reserves will decline by only $150 as a result of the $1,000 reduction in demand deposits. Hence, if a $1,000 reserve deficiency previously existed, an $850 reserve deficiency would then exist, even though it was transferred to another bank. The process of contraction through the *banking system* would have to continue until deposits were reduced by $6,667 before the reserve deficiency would be eliminated, assuming the same 15 per cent reserve requirement ratio as before. Therefore, it is clear that the Federal Reserve System can exert a powerful force for either monetary expansion or monetary contraction depending on whether it is increasing or decreasing the reserves of the commercial banking system.

ANALYSIS OF CHANGES IN SOURCES AND USES OF COMMERCIAL BANK RESERVE FUNDS

The writer has the uncomfortable feeling that the content of this chapter is both tedious and complicated for some, while too elementary for others. There appears to be no easy solution to this dilemma. For those who are confused and/or bored, it may be worthwhile reminding you that the ultimate objective is to forge a method of analysis which will enable you to use monetary change as a useful guide for improving economic and investment timing decisions. It will, hopefully, be worth your time and effort to proceed. Learning is usually a painful process even though ultimately worth the effort. If you have survived so far, read on!

Since changes in deposits result from changes in bank reserves, an understanding of monetary change must be predicated on an analysis of the factors which change bank reserves. Since by far the largest component of the money supply is demand deposits—80 per cent of the total—controlling the money stock is essentially a matter of controlling the volume of deposits. As indicated previously, deposit increases can take place only if banks have excess reserves, and monetary contraction must result if reserves decline and a reserve deficiency develops. It is by influencing the volume of bank reserves that the Federal Reserve exerts control over the stock of money.

In analyzing factors influencing the change in bank reserves, it is useful to think in terms of *sources* of potential reserve funds and *uses* of those funds. If all potential reserve funds were actually used as bank reserves, this approach would not be necessary, but such is not the case. Unfortunately, there are also nonreserve uses of potential reserve funds. A simple equation will serve to illuminate this reserve relation: sources of potential reserve funds = nonreserve uses + bank reserves (reserve uses). Therefore, any net increase in potential reserve funds will be accompanied by a similar increase in the sum of nonreserve and reserve uses, and, conversely, a decrease in potential reserve funds will be accompanied by a decline in the sum of nonreserve uses and reserves. Because of our interest in factors influencing deposits, we are primarily interested in changes in bank reserves, but to understand these changes we must analyze changes in both the sources of potential reserve funds and nonreserve uses.

Data on the total sources and uses of reserve funds are available each week in a Federal Reserve Board release, number XF, *Factors Affecting Member Bank Reserves*. An abbreviated and slightly rearranged table follows, giving average weekly data for the week ending March 27, 1963.

Observe that sources and uses are equal, and that changes in sources and uses are also the same except for rounding errors.

As a result of a 1959 change in banking laws, banks are now allowed to count some of their cash in vault as reserves. Therefore, on the above date it was estimated that member banks had $2,896,000 of vault cash that could be counted as reserves, making a total of $19,586,000. Each commercial bank must keep a specified percentage of its deposits with Federal Reserve banks, and these funds become required reserves. On the above date, members had *required reserves* of $19,108,000. Therefore, *excess reserves* amounted to $478 million.

TABLE 4
SOURCES AND USES OF POTENTIAL COMMERCIAL BANK RESERVES
(Millions of Dollars)
Week ending March 27, 1963

SOURCES		CHANGE FROM	
		Week Ago	Year Ago
Reserve bank credit	$32,555	+ 114	+ 2,434
Gold stock	15,878		— 788
Treasury currency outstanding	5,576	— 1	— 11
Total	$54,009	+ 113	+ 1,635
Uses			
Currency in circulation	$34,415	— 96	+ 1,464
Treasury cash holdings	451	+ 3	+ 18
Treasury deposits with Federal Reserve banks ..	1,014	+ 169	+ 533
Foreign deposits with Federal Reserve banks ...	186	+ 6	— 11
Other deposits with Federal Reserve banks	174	— 17	— 144
Other Federal Reserve accounts (net)	1,078	+ 5	+ 50
Total nonreserve uses	$37,319	+ 71	+ 1,910
Total member bank reserves with Federal Reserve	$16.690	+ 42	— 276
Total uses of potential reserves	$54,009	+ 113	+ 1,634

Source: Board of Governors, Federal Reserve System.

As indicated in Table 4, there are three basic sources of potential reserve funds for commercial banks—Federal Reserve credit, the gold stock, and Treasury currency outstanding. Funds derived from these sources may actually be used as reserves, or they may be utilized for nonreserve purposes. Nonreserve uses of potential reserve funds include usage in the form of currency in circulation, Treasury cash holdings, Treasury deposits with the Federal Reserve, foreign and other deposits with the Federal Reserve, and other Federal Reserve accounts.

Reserve bank credit (Table 4), one source of potential reserves, can be increased through purchases by the Federal Reserve Open Market Committee of U.S. government securities or acceptances, through an increase in borrowings by commercial banks from Federal Reserve banks, or through an increase in float or uncollected balances of checks outstanding. The Federal Reserve Open Market Committee has direct and complete control over the timing and the amount of securities and acceptance bought or sold. The System can affect borrowings by commercial banks from the Federal Reserve banks by variations in the discount rate relative to open market rates and by direct restraints on borrowings at the discount window. It cannot directly affect float which varies with the long-term growth and improvement of the banking and transportation system and with short-run seasonal fluctuations. Therefore, the most important methods available to the Federal Reserve for affecting sources of potential reserve funds is through open market purchases and sales, variation in the discount rate, and direct restraints on borrowing by banks. An increase in either of these sources of potential reserve funds will increase reserves of commercial banks unless an offsetting increase in nonreserve uses occurs.

To clarify the effect of changes in the sources of potential reserve funds, T-account analysis is again helpful. Let us consider first the major variable used for executing monetary policy—open market operations. This variable may be used both for offsetting undesirable short-run seasonal or random influences, and for executing the broader purposes of monetary policy. When the Federal Reserve System, through the New York Federal Reserve Bank, buys a U.S. government security from a government security dealer, it makes payment by a check issued on itself. The dealer then deposits the check and it is presented for payment at the regional Federal Reserve bank. Let us assume a purchase of $1 billion was made in the manner indicated.

TABLE 5
PARTIAL BALANCE SHEET

Federal Reserve Bank

U.S. government securities + $1 billion	Member bank reserve deposit + $1 billion

Commercial Bank

Reserves with Federal Reserve bank + $1 billion	Customer deposit + $1 billion

It is therefore clear that a Federal Reserve open market purchase of $1 billion from a government dealer results in a $1 billion increase in bank reserves and an initial increase of $1 billion in deposits. Assuming an average required reserve ratio of 15 per cent, $850,000 excess reserves were created which would be subject to the ultimate multiple expansion previously described. If the expansion process went to the theoretical limit, there would be an ultimate increase of $6.67 billion in deposits. A purchase by the Open Market Committee of a bankers acceptance would have the same effect. If instead of a purchase of government securities or bankers acceptance a sale were made, reserves would be reduced by $1 billion, and the multiple contraction process would at the limit reduce the money stock by $6.67 billion.

If an increase in Federal Reserve credit occurs as a result of an increase in borrowing by commercial banks from a Federal Reserve bank, reserves go up by the amount of borrowing, but there is no initial increase in the stock of money. Nonetheless, these newly acquired reserves can also be expanded into a $6.67 billion increase in deposits, assuming that $1 billion was borrowed. Banks that find themselves in a deficit reserve position may do one of three things: (1)

liquidate loans or investments. (2) Borrow reserves or "Fed funds" from other banks. (3) Borrow from the Federal Reserve. Decision between the last two choices would depend partly on the two rates of interest. The first alternative would probably be selected if the deficit position were expected to be long lasting, whereas the latter two would usually apply when a temporary deficit was expected. An increase in total reserves within the banking system would occur only when the commercial bank decided to relieve its reserve deficit by borrowing from the regional Federal Reserve bank.

The third and final way in which total Federal Reserve credit outstanding could rise would be by an increase in float. Float occurs when one bank's reserve account with the Federal Reserve is credited for checks sent for collection, prior to the debiting of the reserve account of the bank against which the checks were drawn. Many of the checks sent to the Federal Reserve for collection result in an immediate crediting and debiting of the two commercial banks involved in the transaction. However, all checks are credited to the account of the depositing bank no later than two days after they are received at the Federal Reserve bank, even though some of the checks may not yet have been collected. In other words, one bank's reserve account is increased prior to the compensating decrease in other banks' reserve accounts and, hence, float arises. The reserve credit given for checks not yet collected is labeled float.

As float arises, total member bank reserves also rise by the same amount. Let us assume that bank A receives a $1,000 check (Table 6) written on bank B in a distant town. It credits the account of its depositor, debits "cash items in process of collection," and sends the check to the regional Federal Reserve for collection. The Federal Reserve bank will increase its asset account "cash item in process of collection" and initially increase its liability item "deferred availability cash item" prior to increasing bank A's reserve deposit. Up to this point, no float has developed, but if at the end of two days the check was still not collected, the Federal Reserve bank would reduce the deferred availability item and increase bank A's reserve account. At that point, float would develop, and the banking system would enjoy an increase in total reserves.

However, when the check is collected from bank B, reserves of that bank would be decreased, and total member bank reserves would then be back at the initial level.

TABLE 6
PARTIAL BALANCE SHEET

Federal Reserve Bank

(2) Uncollected cash item + $1,000	Deferred availability + $1,000
(3)	Deferred availability − $1,000 Bank A reserve deposit + $1,000

Commercial Bank A

(1) Cash item in process of collection + $1,000	Deposit + $1,000
(4) Cash item − $1,000 Reserve with Federal Reserve + $1,000	

The second major source of potential reserve funds is the gold stock. Monetary effects of a change in the gold stock are complex. When either freshly mined gold or gold from abroad is sold to the U.S. Treasury, sources of potential reserve funds are expanded by a like amount. Let us assume that the U.S. Treasury purchases $1,000 worth of gold (Table 7), and payment is made by a check drawn on the Treasury's deposit with a Federal Reserve bank. The recipient of the check will deposit it with a commercial bank, and deposits and reserves will go up by $1,000. But in the process of paying for the gold, the U.S. Treasury balances with the Federal

Reserve bank were reduced by $1,000. The Treasury would replenish those funds by issuing a gold certificate to the Federal Reserve for the amount of the purchase, and its deposit account would be increased.

TABLE 7
PARTIAL BALANCE SHEET

U.S. Treasury

(1) Gold + $1,000 Deposit with Federal Reserve bank − $1,000	
(4) Deposit with Federal Reserve bank + $1,000	Gold certificates + $1,000

Federal Reserve Bank

	(3) Member bank reserve deposit + $1,000 U.S. Treasury deposit − $1,000
(5) Gold certificates + $1,000	U.S. Treasury Deposit + $1,000

Commercial Bank

(2) Reserve with Federal Reserve + $1,000	Deposits + $1,000

It is therefore clear that total reserves and deposits have risen in the first instance by the amount of the $1,000 gold purchase. With a 15 per cent reserve requirement, excess reserves would rise by $850 which could be expanded by $6\frac{2}{3}$ times. An outflow of gold would have the opposite effect. Buyers of gold make payment by checks on commercial banks, and the checks are sent to the Federal Reserve bank for collection. Therefore, commercial bank reserves are decreased by the amount of the gold purchases, and Treasury balances are in the first instance increased. But these funds would be used for retiring a like amount of gold certificates held by the Federal Reserve bank. It should be noted that total reserves of the Federal Reserve System are affected by gold flows, whereas they are untouched by changes in Federal Reserve credit.

The gold stock is not normally subject to direct control by the Federal Reserve Board or other government authorities, although gold flows may and frequently are offest by compensating changes in Federal Reserve credit. Gold flows are usually affected by such factors as the size of the deficit in the U.S. balance of payments and the relative preference of foreign central banks for gold vs. dollars. Variations in the gold stock are occasionally important, but on a week-to-week basis they are usually inconsequential. In those periods when gold outflows become a significant factor, the Federal Reserve may alter its open market activities in order to compensate for them unless the resulting altered bank reserves are consistent with current economic policies. A recent example of offsetting Federal Reserve operations occurred during the last half of 1960 when economic policy was directed at halting the recession and generating recovery. Despite the outflow of $1.5 billion gold in the last half of 1960, total bank reserves rose substantially due mainly to Federal Reserve open market purchases of U.S. securities. It should be noted also that in recent years the Federal Reserve has sometimes attempted to affect gold flows directly by supporting short-term interest rates and trading in foreign currency. These efforts have been directed at deterring short-term capital outflows by discouraging speculative activities and by raising short-term interest rates in the U.S. relative to those available abroad.

A third but minor source of potential bank reserves is Treasury currency outstanding. The amount outstanding has increased gradually over time, but short-run changes are small and have minor effects on total bank reserves. Treasury currency consists of coins, silver certificates, and some old currency which is not being generally used but for which the Treasury has redemption responsibility. When the Treasury issues new currency, it is shipped to the Federal Reserve for credit to Treasury deposits. When these resulting deposits are drawn down as the Treasury makes expenditures, an increase in commercial bank reserves will result.

Now let us turn to an analysis of uses of potential reserve funds. One of the most seasonally volatile nonreserve uses is currency in circulation. Although holders of money may draw no sharp distinction between their demand deposits and currency, a transfer in form from deposits to currency has a sharp impact on bank reserves. The public typically acquires cash by "cashing" a check. Suppose a bank customer cashes a $100 check (Table 8) against his account in exchange for currency. Commercial bank deposits decline by $100, and the bank's currency holding is decreased by a like amount. But the currency must be replaced by the bank to meet other customer demands, and this is achieved by ordering currency from the regional Federal Reserve bank and making payment by authorizing a reduction in its reserve balance. The public now has the same amount of money as before, but more is in currency and less in demand deposit form. However, bank reserves have been decreased by $100, and excess reserves have declined by $85, since required reserves slipped $15. Unless more reserves were acquired, the banking system would have to liquidate loans and/or investments and, hence, deposits amounting to $567 ($85 $\times$ 6⅔), assuming a 15 per cent average required reserve ratio.

TABLE 8
Partial Balance Sheet

Commercial Bank		Federal Reserve Bank	
(1) Vault cash — $100	Deposits — $100	(3)	Member bank reserve deposit — $100
(2) Vault cash + $100 Reserve with Federal Reserve — $100			Federal Reserve notes outstanding + $100

When currency is returned to the banking system, the process is reversed. The Federal Reserve must take action frequently to offset the destabilizing influence of currency outflows and inflows. The foregoing analysis, incidentally, provides some insight into the reason for widespread bank failures during the Great Depression when depositors attempted to convert their funds into currency. The resulting reserve deficiency caused forced sale of investments and the calling of loans, and thereby intensified the depression. Fortunately, there has been no modern parallel to that experience, partly because of deposit insurance.

Another nonreserve use of potential reserve funds which is of considerable importance is Treasury deposits with the Federal Reserve. The Treasury makes most payments out of funds on deposit with the Federal Reserve, but the bulk of Treasury funds are on deposit with commercial banks in accounts labeled "tax and loan accounts." Transfers are made regularly from the tax and loan accounts with member banks to Treasury deposits with the Federal Reserve from which most Treasury checks are paid. A transfer of Treasury funds from commercial banks to the Federal Reserve will have an effect similar to the withdrawal of currency from a commercial bank, as indicated in Table 9 which assumes a $1 million transfer. Reserves of commercial banks are reduced

TABLE 9
PARTIAL BALANCE SHEET

Federal Reserve Bank

	Member bank reserve deposits − $1 million U.S. Treasury deposit + $1 million

Commercial Bank

Reserves with F.R. bank − $1 million	U.S. government deposits − $1 million

by the amount of the transfer to the Federal Reserve bank, and excess reserves decline by $850,000 assuming a 15 per cent average required reserve ratio. In the first instance, the money stock is unaffected, however, since Treasury demand deposits held with commercial banks are excluded from the money supply. Due to the potentially disturbing influence of Treasury transfers, special attention is given to attempting to keep Treasury balances with the Federal Reserve fairly uniform. In addition, in recent years such fluctuations have been reduced substantially by daily adjustments in the tax and loan balances at the large commercial banks. The pulling down of Treasury balances with the Federal Reserve resulting from Treasury expenditures in excess of new deposits with the Federal Reserve bank would decrease nonreserve uses and tend to increase commercial bank reserves.

Additional nonreserve uses of potential reserve funds which are of minor importance are Treasury cash holdings, foreign and other deposits in Federal Reserve banks, and other Federal Reserve accounts. The Treasury holds some cash in its own vaults, and changes in these holdings affect member bank reserves in the same manner as changes in the Treasury's deposit account with the Federal Reserve. Foreign central banks, international institutions, and some nonmember banks keep funds on deposit in Federal Reserve banks. These funds usually build up out of funds transferred from member banks and result in a decrease in member bank reserves. When a reverse flow occurs, member bank balances are augmented. Other Federal Reserve accounts represent a combination of the balance sheet items not already considered as separate factors affecting reserves. When this residual dollar figure increases, usually in response to net current earnings of the Reserve banks, bank reserves are reduced. When this factor declines, bank reserves rise.

To recapitulate briefly, the ability of commercial banks to expand loans and investments, deposits, and, hence, the money stock (when the required reserve ratio is fixed) depends on the total reserves and their distribution between required and excess reserves. Potential bank reserves are provided by Federal Reserve credit, the gold stock, and Treasury currency outstanding. These may be used as reserves of commercial banks, or they may go into nonreserve uses. The following simple equations summarize the pertinent relations which determine the ability of commercial banks to expand the stock of money.

1. Sources of potential reserve funds = nonreserve uses + member bank reserves with the Federal Reserve banks.
2. Member bank reserves = reserves with the Federal Reserve banks + cash allowed as reserves.
3. Member bank reserves − required reserves = excess reserves.

Unless commercial banks have either excess reserves or access to them through the discount window, they are unable to further expand the stock of money. For the banking system as a whole, each dollar of excess reserves may be expanded 6⅔ assuming an average reserve requirement of 15 per cent. The expansion of deposits comes about through an increase in total loans and/or investments. With each $1.00 of excess reserves, $6.67 of loans and/or investments may be made before the resulting new deposits will convert the $1.00 of excess reserves into required reserves.

One additional factor should be recognized at this point. The Federal Reserve has the power to increase or decrease the required ratio within limits set by law. By raising the average required reserve ratio, required reserves can be increased, thereby decreasing the amount of excess reserves so long as total reserves are unchanged. A reduction in the average required reserve ratio will increase the supply of excess reserves. Manipulation of the required reserve ratio can, therefore, increase or decrease excess reserves without affecting either the total of potential reserve funds or their uses. Furthermore, the lower the average reserve ratio, the larger the potential multiple expansion of each dollar of excess reserves. As indicated previously, the potential multiple expansion of excess reserves varies directly with the reciprocal of the required reserve ratio, i.e., potential multiple expansion = 1 ÷ the average required reserve ratio.

Since the Federal Reserve System has the power to increase or decrease the total sources of potential reserve funds and also the power to change the average required ratio, it therefore has the power to determine the stock of money. The simple, largely correct, and most relevant observation is that monetary policy as set by the Federal Reserve Board can determine the growth rate of the stock of money, even though the Federal Reserve does not directly control all the factors affecting reserves.

IV

Detecting and Measuring Monetary Change

At this point, the reader is aware that the author's objective is to develop an understanding of a method of analysis which will enable the careful analyst to use monetary change as a guide to improving economic and investment timing decisions. Up to the present, it has been demonstrated that (1) monetary change has a leading and fairly consistent relation to subsequent changes in stock prices and economic activity; (2) a simple explanation utilizing money as the causal variable rationalizes the foregoing relationships; (3) the process of monetary change can be useful if the analyst understands (a) the elementary structure of the banking system, (b) the process of multiple expansion and contraction of money, and (c) the analysis of sources and uses of potential reserve funds. Now that we understand what factors cause money to vary, there remains the important problem of detecting and measuring monetary change. Unfortunately, there is not unanimous agreement as to how this task is best performed. Per-

haps the most obvious approach is to rely on the statements
of Federal Reserve officials concerning current monetary
policy. But while these statements may occasionally provide
a useful explanation of current policy, they cannot be a
substitute for analysis. Federal Reserve officials are generally
reluctant to keep the market informed as to their present
and planned actions. Once a year, the minutes of the Open
Market Committee are published, but they are not available
on a current basis. Speeches by members of the Board of
Governors are available shortly after delivery, and they occasionally provide useful insights into present and planned
policies. But the prudent analyst of money should be more
interested in what monetary authorities are doing than in
what they say they are trying to do, for, unfortunately, there
is not always a one-to-one relation between monetary plans
and results.

MONEY STOCK, THE BEST MEASURE OF MONETARY CHANGE

Since banking data are published promptly and seldom
require extensive revision, there is no shortage of facts. The
problem is one of deciding which facts are most relevant.
The most direct and in many ways the most useful means
of measuring a monetary policy change is that of observing
changes in the stock of money (Chart 2). Data on the daily
average stock of money are available every two weeks in a
Federal Reserve Board release, *Demand Deposits, Currency
and Related Items*, and the money stock as of the last Wednes-
day of the month is available in a release, *Assets and Liabilities of All Banks in the United States*, which will reflect
changes brought about by monetary policy action, both
planned and unplanned, as well as changes resulting from
other forces. Money stock data as of near month end is
frequently distorted by serious random influences not readily

removable. Consequently, the average money stock data are most appropriate for analytical purposes. Nonetheless, near-month-end data sometimes will give a useful clue as to most recent changes. Both releases are issued promptly with a time lag of only about two weeks.

But raw average money stock data alone will not provide the proper tool. To begin with, the usual seasonal influence must be removed from the data so the analyst can determine whether an apparent change is real or merely seasonal in nature. Fortunately, money stock data are reported in both raw and seasonally adjusted form.

Further adjustment is necessary if the data are to be of maximum usefulness. In addition to the seasonal and random influences which affect the magnitude of monetary change, there is also a long-term or secular growth trend and the cyclical trend. The cyclical changes in the monetary series are most useful for our purposes. Frequently, the stock of money grows both in periods of business expansion and contraction. Although the money stock has inevitably declined in deep depressions, it has frequently continued to rise in mild recessions, although not always. For example, there was a moderate absolute decline in the stock of money from mid-1959 to mid-1960 prior to the mildest recession in the post-war period. However, the money stock began expanding in the first month of business contraction, somewhat sooner with respect to the upper turning point of the business cycle than is typically the case.

Even though the money stock may rise during recessions, this may not mean there is no relation between monetary change and the business cycle. It may merely mean the secular upward trend is stronger than the cyclical trend, so that the latter is not readily apparent in the seasonally adjusted data. Therefore, a method of removing the long-term trend must be adopted.

The two most common ways of eliminating the secular trend from the cyclical pattern in time series data are to express the data in terms of deviations from trend or to compute the rate of change in the data. Although rates of change often yield a rather erratic or choppy series, they do not require a decision about the kind of trend to fit or the period to cover. Furthermore, the observations for any particular period do not depend on far distant observations for other periods that affect fitted trends. Also, the series can be extended backward or forward without either recomputing or extrapolating trends. The trend adjustment chosen in this book is the computation of rates of change in the stock of money.[1] An economic factor conditioning the choice is that monetary authorities may readily alter the secular trend in the stock of money as conditions change. It is therefore desirable to allow for a trend that can shift drastically over time, and rate-of-change computations do this.

One final adjustment to the data appears warranted if the resulting series is to be operational, provided the reader is not convinced that all meaning has already been adjusted out of the raw monetary data. Ideally, it would be desirable to have a rate-of-change series which is both smooth and highly sensitive to recent changes in the money stock. Unfortunately we cannot have both. In the real world of practical data manipulation, the analyst is frequently faced with unpleasant choices between competing desires that must be compromised. Such is the present case. The analyst can have a highly sensitive but erratic series by computing the annual

---

[1] In the monetary research by Milton Friedman, the rate-of-change adjustment was adopted, but another authority, Clark Warburton, chose deviations from a fitted trend: See Milton Friedman, "The Relationship of Prices to Economic Stability and Growth" (U.S. Congress Joint Economic Committee Document No. 23734), pp. 241–56; "The Lag in Effect of Monetary Policy," *Journal of Political Economy*, October, 1961, especially pp. 453–54; Clark Warburton, "The Volume of Money and the Price Levels between World Wars," *Journal of Political Economy*, June, 1945, pp. 153–54.

rate of growth each month; that is, compute the percentage change from the preceding month and annualize by multiplying the resultant percentage by 12.

At the other extreme, an annualized percentage change from the same month a year ago will yield a relatively smooth curve but one that is rather insensitive to recent changes. The resulting percentage change data will be influenced not only by the recent change but also by the level existing one year ago. A reasonable compromise results from computing a current annualized rate of change for each month but averaging the most recent six months' rates. The resulting series removes most short-run erratic movements but retains fair sensitivity to average recent developments. For those reasons, the six-month moving average is the series used in subsequent charts reflecting monetary growth. Nonetheless, an analyst should not become a slave to the particular form of arithmetical computation adopted. Hence, the most sensitive series also should be computed and analyzed in detecting most recent fluctuations in monetary growth.[2]

In detecting and measuring monetary change, the ultimate answer as to what is happening to the nation's liquidity is provided by measuring the rate of monetary change in the manner indicated above. This technique has the advantage of being simple, direct, and timely, and for most purposes provides both a necessary and sufficient measure.

MEASURING CHANGES IN TOTAL RESERVES

But a careful current analysis of sources and uses of potential reserves can frequently provide useful supplementary information. Analysis of changes in the individual items making up the sources and uses of potential reserve funds is

---

[2] See Appendix A for further elaboration

difficult because of short-run seasonal and random fluctuations. For example, a significant increase in Federal Reserve purchases of U.S. government securities in the last half of the year may or may not indicate an expansive monetary policy. Substantial seasonal increases of money in circulation requires offsetting action by the Federal Reserve if there is to be no contraction in deposits. Gold flows into or out of the nation may also require offsetting action by the monetary authority. Since it is extremely difficult for the human mind to evaluate correctly the impact of several simultaneously changing variables, it is much more useful to concentrate attention on total bank reserves. Total bank reserves reflect the net effect on reserves of all changes in the sources and non-reserve uses of potential reserve funds. As pointed out previously, changes in total bank reserves is the most important factor determining the ability of banks to change loans and investment totals and, hence, the stock of money.

However, if changes in total bank reserves are to provide useful information, this series also must be substantially adjusted. The usual seasonal movement must be removed from the series so the analyst can determine when an apparent change is of basic significance or merely seasonal in nature. Prior to removing the seasonal influences, however, a more basic adjustment is necessary. As indicated previously, the Federal Reserve can increase excess reserves either by increasing total reserves or by reducing the required reserve ratio, thereby reducing required reserves. Therefore, if the total reserve series is to properly reflect the ability of the banking system to expand bank credit and, hence, the stock of money, the historical series must be adjusted for changes in required reserves. Although the Federal Reserve frequently adjusts total reserves by increasing the total sources of potential reserves created, changes in the required reserve ratio are infrequent, hence, the adjustment problem posed is minor. Fortunately, the reserve data is reported in fully adjusted form on a biweekly basis by the St. Louis Federal Reserve Bank in a release entitled *Bank Reserves and Money*.[3]

In fact, fully adjusted data is presented by the St. Louis Federal Reserve on four different reserve series: (1) Total Reserves of Member Banks, (2) Total Reserves of Member Banks Less Reserves behind Treasury Deposits, (3) Reserves Required to Support Privately Held Deposits, and (4) Reserves Available for Private Demand Deposits. The four series become more narrow in coverage from one through four, and each is appropriate for achieving a somewhat different kind of understanding. Series number 1 is unambiguous and provides a fully adjusted total reserve series for all member banks. But Treasury deposits are not a part of the money stock as usually defined, since they are not privately held. Therefore, series 2 subtracts out reserves behind Treasury deposits. Since Treasury deposits sometimes change substantially, the resulting series provides a better measure of reserves available to support the private money stock. Series number 3 subtracts excess reserves and gives a good measure of actual required reserves to support privately held deposits. Finally, series 4 eliminates reserves against time deposits from series 2, and therefore, provides a measure of reserves available for private demand deposits, the most important component of the money stock. Chart 2 contains series 2, 3, and 4, since they are the ones most closely related to changes in the stock of money. Comparison of the rate of growth in the money stock and the rate of growth in required reserves (Chart 2) indicates a reasonably close relation exists.

Even so, the relation is not perfect. There are several reasons why some discrepancy exists between various reserve series and the stock of money.[4] A shift between private deposits

---

[3] In an article in the July, 1963, issue of the *Federal Reserve Bulletin* entitled "Measures of Member Bank Reserves," historical data on several reserve series were presented and discussed.

[4] For an elaborate discussion, see *Review*, St. Louis Federal Reserve Bank, March, 1962, pp. 5–11.

CHART 2
Member Bank Reserves and Monetary Growth

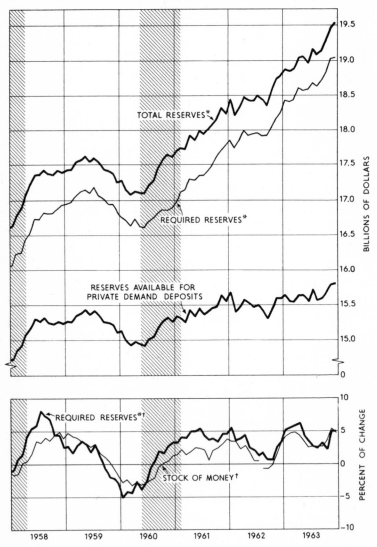

Source: Federal Reserve System. Daily average figures adjusted for seasonal and reserve
requirement changes.
  *Reserves of member banks less reserves behind Treasury deposits.
  †Annual rate of monthly change, six-month moving average.
  Shaded periods are contractions in business activity.
  Data presented in Appendix B.

and U.S. Treasury deposits in commercial banks results in a change in the money stock but not in total reserves. Therefore, series number 1 would be misleading, but the other three would not. Changes in excess reserves, which are under the control of the commercial banks, also cause divergences between total reserves and the stock of money and between total reserves of member banks less reserves behind Treasury deposits and the money stock, as well as between reserves available for private demand deposits and the money stock. Series 3 would be unaffected, since excess reserves are already removed from the data. Banks generally try to keep excess reserves at a low working level since they are a nonearning asset, but the level may fluctuate as much as $200 million to $300 million over the business cycle in response to changes in short-term interest rates and the demand for bank credit.

Movements of deposits between classes of banks which have a different required reserve ratio behind demand deposits may also cause a lack of correspondence between reserve changes and money stock changes. For example, central reserve city banks and reserve city banks have a required reserve ratio of 16.5 per cent, whereas country banks are required to keep 12 per cent on reserve. This discrepancy would apply to all four series, since in effect the deposit shift represents a change in the average required reserve ratio which are assumed to be unchanged in each of the series.

The movement of funds from time deposits to demand deposits or vice versa has a somewhat similar effect, since the required reserve ratio is considerably less for time deposits, only 4 per cent, and the shift in effect changes the average required reserve ratio. Although time deposits have on average grown faster than demand deposits over a long period of time, the relative shift was so gradual that little distortion between reserves and total deposit growth resulted. However, on two occasions in recent years the shift was substantial, and the resulting distortion was considerable. At the beginning of 1957 and again at the beginning of 1962, the Federal Reserve Board raised the ceiling rate that commercial banks could pay on time money. The increase was from 2.5 per cent to 3 per cent or an increase of 20 per cent in the first case, and from 3 to 4 per cent or an increase of 30 per cent in 1962. Many banks promptly increased the rate paid, and there was a large inflow of funds into commercial bank time deposits. To an unknown extent, there was a shift from demand deposits to time deposits within commercial banks and also a shift of liquid assets from other forms to time deposits. Also, the savers shifted the allocation of the current flow of savings toward commercial banks. Due to the reduction in the average required reserve ratio resulting from the shift, it was possible for commercial banks to substantially expand loans and investments even though total reserves did not expand commensurately. As indicated in Chart 3, total reserves of commercial banks declined slightly in 1962 into the early fall months when an expansion occurred. Total required reserves reflected approximately the same trend, while reserves available for private demand deposits declined sharply into fall, thereby forcing the decline that occurred in demand deposits.

Changes in demand deposits of nonmember banks cause a change in the stock of money without a change in reserves. Although demand deposits of nonmember banks are included in the money stock, changes in these deposits may occur without a change in member bank reserves, since legal reserves of nonmember banks are not required to be in the same form as those of member banks.

Too, a change in interbank balances will result in a distortion between reserve changes and changes in the money stock. When a country member bank transfers deposits from its account with the Federal Reserve bank to its city correspondent bank, the reserve requirement against those funds rises to 16.5 per cent. For the banking system as a whole, excess reserves will decline and monetary contraction will result even though total reserves are unchanged.

Finally, movements of currency into and out of banks will affect both reserves and money, but not in equal proportions. As pointed out in the analysis of sources and uses of potential reserve funds, a movement of currency into banks adds to bank reserves. Based on these newly acquired reserves, the banking system can expand credit and deposits. But the deposit expansion is partially offset by a contraction in the currency component of the money supply. Thus, the net expansion in the stock of money would be less than if the increase in reserves had come from other sources. An outflow of currency will produce a reduction in reserves but will cause a smaller initial contraction of the money stock than if the reserve reduction were induced by another factor, since the resulting contraction is partially offset by the increase in the currency component of money. Shifts in the composition of the stock of money between currency and deposits tend to be of very modest proportions in most cases, and it would be only in periods of "bank panics" similar to the early 1930's that this factor would be of great importance. Existence of deposit insurance substantially reduces the risk of such an occurrence.

Despite the above qualifications concerning the potential imperfections in the relation between bank reserves and the stock of money, the actual resulting distortions are generally of small magnitude and usually can be ignored. It is nonetheless important that the analyst be aware of these potential distortions so he may avoid being a victim of the system of analysis on those very few occasions when one of the above disturbances develops.

FREE RESERVES—THE CONVENTIONAL BUT
UNRELIABLE MEASURE

The most frequently used but least reliable measure of monetary policy as it affects monetary expansion is free reserves[5] (Chart 3). Free reserves or net borrowed reserves are defined as excess reserves minus borrowings of commercial banks from the Federal Reserve System. It is the free reserve concept which is most regularly referred to by bankers, financial writers, and even by representatives of the Federal Reserve. The reason for the almost exclusive reliance on free reserves as a measure of monetary policy is difficult to understand in view of its many important limitations. Its popularity may be due to familiarity and its availability in the financial press each Friday morning. Perhaps the basic explanation for its persistent popularity is lack of widespread understanding of the severe limitations of free reserves or net borrowed reserves as a measure of monetary change. It is readily apparent that free reserves fluctuate with the business cycle in an approximate range from about —$500 million in the last part of a business expansion to about +$500 million during recession periods. The cyclical swing in free reserves is due to changes in both excess reserves and borrowings, but primarily in borrowings. Excess reserves tend to increase in recession periods when lower interest rates reduce the incentive for banks to keep all their excess funds fully loaned or invested. During periods of rising economic activity and higher interest rates, excess reserves are kept near the operating minimum. On the other hand, borrowings from Federal Reserve banks decrease sharply during recession periods, since

---

[5] For an excellent definitive theoretical and statistical discussion of the relation between free reserves and the stock of money see: A. James Meigs, *Free Reserves and the Money Supply* (Chicago: University of Chicago Press, 1962).

the opportunities for borrowing and loaning the funds at a higher rate are substantially reduced. As economic activity improves, credit demands increase, and interest rates rise relative to the discount rate, borrowing again becomes profitable and the volume of borrowing sharply increases. Even though it was profitable to do so, an individual bank probably would not borrow from the Federal Reserve bank for long periods of time because of fear that the Federal Reserve would exercise its "right" to deny credit. However, the elimination of an overinvested position by sale of securities and repayment to the Federal Reserve by an individual bank would merely transfer the deficit reserve position to another

CHART 3
RESERVE POSITION

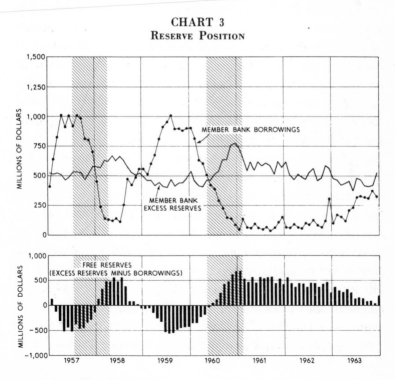

Source: Federal Reserve Board.
Shaded periods are contractions in business activity.
Data presented in Appendix B.

bank which would have an incentive to borrow from the Federal Reserve. Therefore, it is possible for the banking system to build up its indebtedness to the Federal Reserve System as it becomes more profitable to do so, even though no single bank is motivated by the profit incentive only.

But why are free reserve changes a misleading guide to understanding monetary policy? Of prime importance is the fact that free reserves are not closely correlated with either adjusted total bank reserves or the stock of money and, hence, usually do not provide a proper clue to understanding liquidity changes. The reason for the poor relation is that any given level of free reserves is consistent with either monetary expansion, stability, or contraction. Free reserves concentrate attention on only two of the many factors affecting the ability of the banking system to either expand or contract credit and the stock of money. Borrowing from the Federal Reserve is one of the sources of potential reserve funds, thus, an increase in borrowings tends to raise total bank reserves, but an increase in borrowings tends to reduce free reserves and suggests monetary restriction. Conversely, a reduction in borrowings from the Federal Reserve tends to reduce the reserves in the banking system and exerts a restrictive effect on monetary expansion; yet free reserves are thereby increased, so this measure suggests an expansive monetary trend. Also, an increase in excess reserves will increase free reserves but will reduce the amount of deposits that a given level of total reserves will support. Many factors other than free reserves affect the ability of banks to expand and contract deposits, and the single series that reflects most of them is adjusted total reserves of banks.

Meigs[6] persuasively argues that the most fruitful hypothesis concerning free reserves is that banks seek to maintain certain

---

[6] *Ibid.* Especially Chaps. 1, 4, and 6.

desired ratios of excess reserves and borrowing (or free reserves) to total deposits. He demonstrates that these desired ratios depend on the market rate of interest and the discount rate, since these are the major factors influencing profitability of loan and investment decisions. The higher the market rate of interest, the lower will be the banking system's desired level of free reserves. The higher the market interest rates relative to the discount rate, the higher will be the banking system's desired level of borrowing from Federal Reserve banks. Higher market rates of interest tends to lower desired excess reserves, since the cost of maintaining idle funds increases. As interest rates and the amount of reserves change, the actual ratios depart from the desired ratios. In trying to adjust the actual reserve ratios to the desired ratios, banks increase or decrease loans and investments, thus causing deposits to change.

There tends to be a considerable lag between an apparent change in monetary policy as measured by free reserves and the reflection of the change in the rate of growth of the stock of money. Although the length of the lag can be determined in hindsight, it can be determined when it is happening only by focusing attention on adjusted total reserves of banks. The slippage between changing free reserves and changing monetary growth arises because of institutional and market factors; namely, the existence of a discount mechanism whereby banks can, at their own initiative, borrow additional reserve funds or pay off debts to the Federal Reserve, and the ability of banks independently to vary the volume of excess reserves.

During a business expansion, interest rates usually tend to rise relative to the discount rate as the demands for credit by private borrowers increase. In such conditions, the Federal Reserve Board, when operating a flexible monetary policy, usually restricts the volume of reserve funds through open market sales of securities. Banks tend to increase their borrowing from the Federal Reserve as interest rates rise relative to the discount rate. Since banks are in business for profit, they are inclined to concentrate their borrowing from the Federal Reserve at a time when it is advantageous from a profit point of view to do so. Also, excess reserves tend to decline in such periods, since banks tend to keep their funds fully invested when it is costly in terms of foregone returns to maintain a high level of excess reserves on which they receive no interest.

When monetary policy is eased, presumably when the economy begins a descent into a recession, the Federal Reserve System may provide additional reserves, but at the same time the demand for money declines, and interest rates usually drop relative to the discount rate. The typical reaction of the banking system is first to pay off debt to the Federal Reserve since it is less profitable, and banks also attempt to restore the liquidity that was reduced during the boom phase. Since the demand for money is reduced and interest rates typically decline relative to the discount rate, it becomes less profitable to borrow from the Federal Reserve, and borrowing is reduced, thereby reducing total reserves. Further, there is at the same time a tendency in the banking system to allow excess reserves to rise as a result of the reduced profitability of investing marginal funds.

These adjustments mean that even though the Federal Reserve may be providing additional funds to the banking system, adjusted total bank reserves may be growing less rapidly or even declining. Hence, we find the anomalous situation wherein an increase in the amount of reserve funds provided directly by the Federal Reserve System does not lead to an immediate increase in total bank reserves, bank assets, and thus the money stock. The length of the time lag prior to an increase in the stock of money will depend on how vigorously the Federal Reserve pursues its easy-money policy and how rapidly commercial banks pay off debt and raise excess reserves. Eventually, the liquidity needs of the banking system will be met, outstanding loans from Federal Reserve banks will approach zero, and excess reserves will be sufficiently high to impel the lending or investment of additional funds. Since a period of declining business activity will be characterized by a declining loan trend, investments must rise more rapidly than loans are declining before the total money stock increases. Although textbook writers are fond of pointing out that expansion and contraction in bank loans brings change in the money stock it is perhaps worthwhile to note in passing that it is usually changes in bank investments that account for both the upper and lower turning points in the money stock growth rate series.

Recent history reveals several examples of the possible misleading indications given by changes in free reserves when unsupported by comparisons with adjusted total reserves and the stock of money. In early 1960, free reserves increased substantially, several months in advance of the May business cycle peak. However, at the same time, adjusted total reserves were declining sharply as was the stock of money. The free reserve improvement occurred primarily because of a reduction in outstanding loans from the Federal Reserve System. Thus, commercial bank debt reduction lowered the reserves available to the banking system, and the total reserve figure indicates that this reduction was not initially offset by other factors which provided reserve funds. It was not until the second quarter of 1960 that adjusted total reserves began to rise rapidly, and shortly thereafter monetary expansion began. This expansion continued throughout the 1960 period of rapid gold outflow, even though an outflow of gold tends to reduce bank reserves and the stock of money. Monetary expansion continued only because the Federal Reserve more than offset the adverse monetary effects of the gold outflow as evidenced by a continued rise in adjusted total reserves.

During 1961, free reserves held steady near the $500 million level throughout the year. However, during the year both mone-

tary expansion and contraction occurred. Adjusted total reserves began a modest contraction during the first quarter and
declined until August, when a sharp rise began. It is not
surprising that changes in the stock of money during 1961
displayed the same patern, after allowing for a slight lag.
Monetary growth ceased in the first quarter of 1961 and declined slightly until September, when a sharp further expansion
began which carried throughout the balance of the year. The
same pattern occurred in 1962. In the latter part of 1963 the
rate of growth of the money stock rose despite a decline in
free reserves.

Although typically the reasons for either a rapid expansion
or contraction in the money stock is found in the underlying
production and employment trends in the domestic economy,
such does not appear to be the case in 1961 and 1962. Due to
increasing concern over the deficit in the balance of payments,
the Federal Reserve attempted to execute monetary policy without placing undue downward pressure on the U.S. Treasury bill
rate which might initiate or accelerate a gold outflow. During
the last part of the year, the normal seasonal pressures on short-
term interest rates are upward. Therefore, it was possible in
1961 and 1962 to substantially increase total bank reserves in
the last few months of the year without causing bill rates to
decline. This was accomplished without significant fluctuations
in free reserves, since the new reserve funds provided were
promptly loaned or invested.

It is clear from the above analysis and examples that early
changes in the supply of reserves made available by the Federal
Reserve System in either the beginning of a recession or the
beginning of an expansion phase of a business cycle will be
offset temporarily by action taken by the banking system.
Hence, even though free reserves may change, there will be no
immediate effect on monetary growth. To the extent that the
Federal Reserve Board takes aggressive offsetting action in the

beginning phase of a policy change, the time required for effecting a change in the money stock will be reduced. So long as the Federal Reserve limits early changes to modest amounts, which appears to have been past policy, a considerable slippage will remain. On other occasions when there is no financial incentive for varying free reserves, a change in reserves provided by the Federal Reserve may result in a prompt change in monetary growth.

CONCLUSIONS

The statement that the Federal Reserve can determine the rate of growth of the stock of money appears to be approximately correct, since the Federal Reserve can determine total reserves. It should be recognized, however, that during the beginning phase of a policy change some slippage is introduced as a result of the reaction of the private banking system unless the Federal Reserve moves aggressively to offset commercial bank action. Some analysts have argued that Federal Reserve action alone cannot increase the stock of money, since the final step can be accomplished only if the banking system utilizes the reserves made available. Even though this statement is technically correct, it must be recognized that the profit incentive provides considerable assurance that additional reserve funds will be utilized for either loans or investments, and therefore the stock of money will respond.

A monetary analyst often can predict changes in the money stock by a careful analysis of current Federal Reserve policy, since the facts relating to Federal Reserve policy are made available weekly, and seasonally adjusted data on total reserves are available every two weeks. Therefore, even though the Federal Reserve does not have direct control over all the factors which affect reserves of banks, it does have the power to create or destroy sufficient sources of potential reserve funds to bring about any effect it may desire on total reserves of member banks.

For example, through the sale of government securities held in March, 1963, the Federal Reserve could reduce sources of reserve funds by about $30.5 billion which would tend to reduce total reserves by a like amount. If reserve requirements were raised to the statutory maximum of 22 per cent for reserve city banks and 14 per cent for country banks, required reserves would be increased from the approximate $19 billion in effect in February, 1963, to $24.27 billion for a rise of about $5.25 billion. Required reserves for reserve city banks would rise from $12.56 billion to $16.72 billion, while country bank required reserves would increase from $6.45 billion to $7.55 billion. In other words, open market sales of government securities plus an increase in required reserve ratios to the statutory maximum would be capable of creating a combined reserve deficit of about $35.75 billion.

Conversely, under the present statutory 25 per cent required gold certificate reserve ratio and with excess gold certificates of $3.5 billion, the System can buy about $14.0 billion of securities and thereby increase the source of potential reserves by that amount. Also, by lowering reserve requirements to the legal minimum of 7 per cent for country banks and 10 per cent for reserve city banks, it can reduce required reserves to $10.5 billion from the present $17.5 billion for a decrease of $7.0 billion. In other words, with present facilities the Federal Reserve Board can increase excess reserves by about $21.0 billion.

It is therefore clear the Federal Reserve has sufficient power at present to offset any extraneous influence on the reserves of the banking system that it considers undesirable. It should be kept in mind that for each $1.00 of excess reserves created by the Federal Reserve System, the commercial banking system can bring about a 6⅔-fold increase in assets and deposits with present average reserve requirements. If the required reserve ratios were lowered to the statutory minimum, the expansion ratio would be about 11 to 1, whereas with maximum required reserve ratios, the expansion ratio would be only 5¼ to 1. Conversely, for each $1.00 of reserves destroyed, commercial banks will be forced to bring about a 6⅔-fold decrease in the money stock with present average reserve requirements, an 11¼-fold decrease with minimum reserve requirements, and a 5¼-fold decrease with maximum reserve ratios. Therefore, the Federal Reserve has sufficient power to bring about any change it deems desirable in the total stock of money.

The monetary analyst can best detect and measure the effects of monetary policy action by reviewing policy statements of Federal Reserve officials, and by observing current changes in the stock of money, adjusted total bank reserves, and, to a lesser extent, free reserves. Statements by officials will sometimes provide a clue as to what their policy is attempting to accomplish, but careful analysis of change in the stock of money will provide the best guide as to the actual net effect of monetary actions. Analysis of current monetary policy actions must always be made in the context of current economic trends. Perhaps the most pertinent question the analyst should ask is, "What monetary action would I take in present circumstances if I were the Federal Reserve Board and had its view on the effect of monetary policy as evidenced in past writing and performance?" If the above approaches are applied constantly, an observer will always be well informed on current monetary developments and will frequently be in a position to predict with considerable accuracy future major changes in monetary trends.

V

The Business Cycle and Indicator Analysis

DESCRIPTION OF CYCLICAL CHANGE

FREQUENT REFERENCE has been made previously to the business cycle. It is worth the slight diversion to examine its nature explicitly. Since both stock price fluctuations and modern monetary policy formulation and execution are influenced by the trend of the business cycle, an understanding of its basic characteristics will facilitate comprehension of the central thesis of this text.

Economists have long been concerned with analysis and prescription for prevention of the U.S. business cycle. Reason for this long-standing interest and concern is accounted for by the economic cost of business fluctuations both in terms of the burdens of inflation on the one hand and unrealized production and income on the other, as well as the human misery and deprivation associated with those events. The group of economists who have produced the largest and probably the most significant body of literature on this important subject is the one that has been associated with the National Bureau of Economic Research. Since its founding in 1920, the NBER has been primarily under the intellectual influence of first Wesley C. Mitchell and then Arthur F. Burns. This chapter will attempt to summarize some of the most significant findings of NBER studies of the business cycle.[1]

The "business cycle" concept results from the study of the sequence of economic events observed in the movements of economic activity. Unfortunately, each business cycle has many unique aspects, but there is sufficient similarity to justify reference to the business cycle. During periods of business expansion, most aggregate economic series increase, but as the expansion continues, limiting forces tend to gain strength until a reversal occurs and a recession begins. Similarly, as a recession develops maturity, forces making for recovery emerge and finally become dominant, and another expansion ensues. The NBER has dated the month of peaks and troughs of U.S. business cycles from 1854 to 1961. During that period, business expansions prevailed about 60 per cent of the time, and economic contractions occurred nearly 40 per cent of the time. If war periods are excluded, business contractions extend to about 44 per cent of the total. There are a total of 26 business contractions if each of the brief downturns shortly following World Wars I and II are counted. If these two are omitted, because of the special circumstances surrounding transition from wartime to peacetime economies, there are 24, and four of them occurred in the post-World War II period.

Although individual business cycles will vary in detail,

---

[1] For a detailed listing of publications see the 43rd Annual Report of the National Bureau of Economic Research, May, 1963.

Arthur F. Burns once described the characteristic movements of economic series during business cycles as follows:[2]

> Let us then take our stand at the bottom of a depression and watch events as they unfold. Production characteristically rises in the first segment of expansion; so do employment and money income; and so do commodity prices, imports, domestic trade, security transactions. Indeed, every series moves upward except bond yields and bankruptcies. In the second stage the broad advance continues, though it is checked at one point—the bond market where trading begins to decline. Bond prices join bond sales in the next stage; in other words, long-term interest rates—which fell during the first half of expansion—begin to rise. In the final stretch of expansion, declines become fairly general in the financial sector. Share trading and stock prices move downward; the liabilities of business failures, which hitherto have been receding, move up again; security issues and construction contracts drop; the turnover of bank deposits slackens; and bank clearings in New York City, though not as yet in the interior, become smaller.
>
> These adverse developments soon engulf the economic system as a whole, and the next stage of the business cycle is the first stage of contraction. Production, employment, commodity prices, personal incomes, business profits—indeed, practically all processes . . . decline. Of course, the liabilities of business failures continue to rise which merely attests the sweep of depression. Long-term interest rates also maintain their rise. But in the next stage the downward drift of bond prices ceases; that is, the rise in long-term interest rates is arrested. By the middle of contraction, bond sales join the upward movement of bond prices. More important still, the liabilties of business failures begin declining, which signifies that the liquidation of distressed business firms has passed its worst phase. These favorable developments are reinforced in the following stage. Share trading and prices revive; business incorporations, security issues, and construction contracts move upward; money begins to turn over more rapidly; even total money payments expand. Before long the expansion spreads to production, employment, prices, money incomes, and domestic trade. But this is already the initial stage of general expansion—the point at which our hurried observation of the business cycle started.

---

[2] See Arthur F. Burns, *New Facts on Business Cycles* (National Bureau of Economic Research 30th Annual Report) (New York, 1950), pp. 3–31; reprinted in *Business Cycle Indicators*, Vol. I (Princeton, N.J.: Princeton University Press, 1961), pp. 13–44.

LEADING, COINCIDENT, AND LAGGING INDICATORS

Although facts will not speak for themselves, it is important that an analyst be aware of the typical factual pattern of a business cycle. This knowledge will be of aid in properly determining the current stage of the business cycle and, hence, will sometimes be of use in anticipating future developments. If facts are to be of maximum benefit, they must be interpreted within the framework of an internally consistent and thoroughly tested theory. Unfortunately, there is no shortage of business cycle theories as any text book on business cycles will demonstrate, but there is a scarcity of tested theories. In order to devise a useful theory consistent with the known facts, it is useful to know those facts. NBER economists have rendered yeoman service in documenting factual trends in the U.S. business cycle over the past century. As might be expected, they found that the turning points of various economic series were not the same, but what is more important, they found that most economic series could be usefully grouped into leading, coincident, and lagging categories. The Department of Commerce issues a monthly publication entitled *Business Cycle Developments* which reports in detail on current trends in the indicators to be discussed as well as many additional series.[3]

The aggregate economic series most frequently followed by business analysts are included in the coincident grouping. Among the coincident series are such broad measures of economic activity as gross national product, industrial production, employment, personal income, retail sales, bank debits, and wholesale prices. It is these approximately coincident indicators that are used primarily in defining the peaks and troughs

---

[3] For a detailed discussion of the indicator approach to business cycle analysis see: Julius Shiskin, *Signals of Recession and Recovery.* (National Bureau of Economic Research Occasional Paper No. 77) (New York, October, 1961).

of business cycles. Each coincident indicator does not perfectly coincide with the peaks and troughs of economic activity as determined by NBER, but each comes close, and some kind of composite of these indicators would more nearly do so. Although industrial production probably most faithfully defines the business cycle, it is important that many coincident indicators be followed if a realistic picture of the current business trend is to emerge. Charts 4, 4*A*, and 4*B*, exerpted from *Business Cycle Developments*, reflect recent cyclical trends in several of these indicators.

Research by the NBER has established that certain economic indicators move in advance or portend changes in the general level of economic activity. These foreshadowing series are called leading indicators. Many of the series are closely related to future production, employment, and income creation. The leading indicators include such series as new orders for durable goods, construction contract awards, inventory change, net new businesses, average hours worked, net corporate profits, and common stock prices. Although no particular series has inevitably led peaks and troughs of economic activity or even led most turns by a consistent number of months, nonetheless, leading indicators have led cyclical turns most of the time, and some tend to have longer average leads than others. Charts 5, 5*A*, 5*B*, 5*C*, and 5*D*, also exerpted from *Business Cycle Developments*, present the cyclical pattern of many leading indicators in recent periods.

Finally, certain economic series are slow to adjust to the mainstream of economic activity. In other words, they tend to lag behind both the advance signals and the coincident indicators and, consequently, are called lagging indicators. They include such factors as labor costs per unit of output, bank interest rates, inventories of finished goods, and consumer debt. Many of the laggers include cost factors which when they increase lead to decreased business profitability and, hence, re-

CHART 4

BUSINESS CYCLE SERIES: 1948 TO PRESENT

NBER Roughly Coincident Indicators

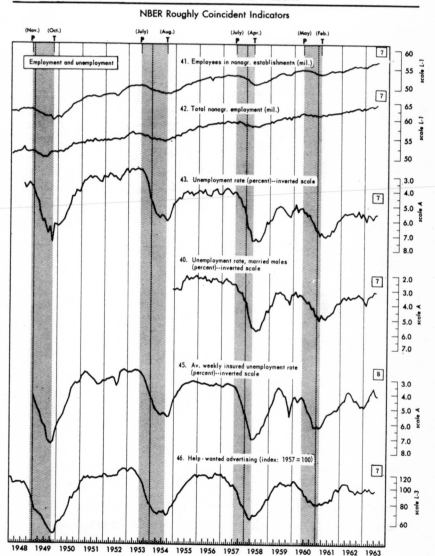

CHART 4*A*

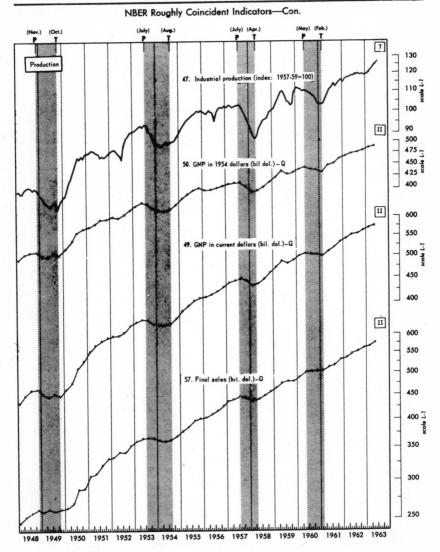

CHART 4B

BUSINESS CYCLE SERIES: 1948 TO PRESENT—Con.

NBER Roughly Coincident Indicators—Con.

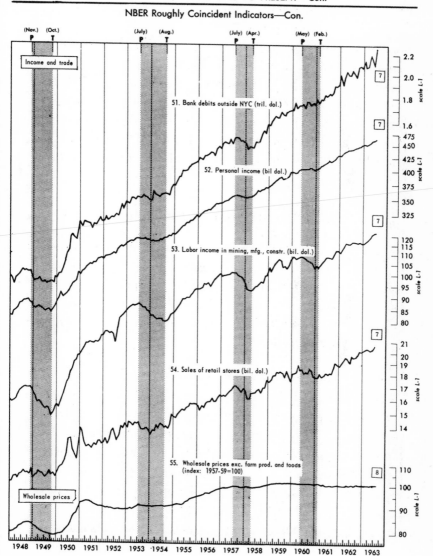

duce the incentive for increasing such business activities as placing new orders and executing expansion plans. Chart 6, which appears regularly in *Business Cycle Developments*, presents some of the laggers.

Regrettably, few of the indicators fit invariably into the simple categories of leading, coincident, and lagging indicators. Therefore, such a classification tends to be somewhat of an oversimplification. However, there is sufficient consistency over many business cycles to make the above classification a useful one. Table 10 gives the average lead or lag of the 26 indicators found to have the most consistent relation in past business cycles.

RATIONALE UNDERLYING THE LEADING INDICATORS

Unfortunately, there appears to be no simple and cohesive economic theory which unifies the various aspects of the indicator approach. However, it is possible to explain many of the observed patterns in a manner that will tend to increase confidence that future patterns with regard to business cycles will be similar to past behavior.[4]

Average Hours Worked per Week, Manufacturing

Since manufacturing industries are more prone to be cyclically sensitive than other industries, the lead nature of various employment and order series are most evident in this industry. Since it is typically less costly to adjust the workweek than to reduce the number of employed, the length of the workweek typically leads employment. Business operates in an uncertain environment. Reductions in the workweek are more readily reversed if orders improve than would be layoffs. Reductions in the workweek enable the employer to keep his labor force intact for future use, whereas layoffs may be unavailable when

---

[4] *Business Cycle Indicators*, Vol. I, pp. 63–69.

CHART 5

BUSINESS CYCLE SERIES: 1948 TO PRESENT

NBER Leading Indicators

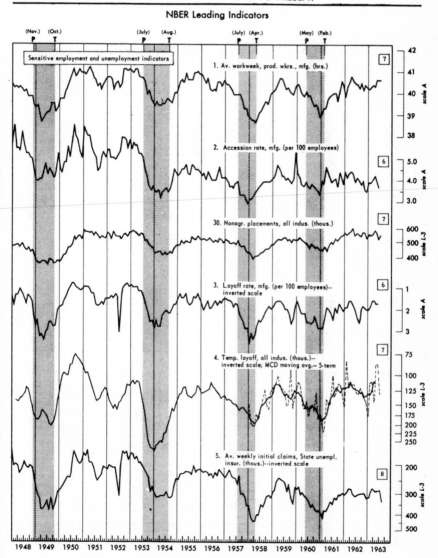

CHART 5A

BUSINESS CYCLE SERIES: 1948 TO PRESENT—Con.

NBER Leading Indicators—Con.

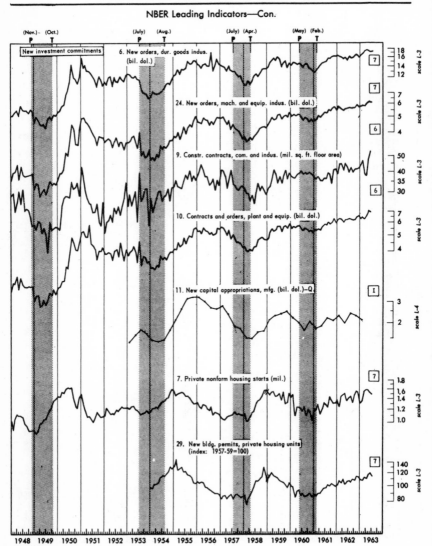

CHART 5B

BUSINESS CYCLE SERIES: 1948 TO PRESENT—Con.

NBER Leading Indicators—Con.

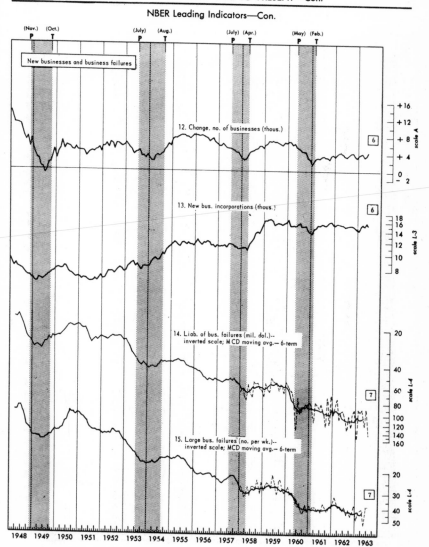

CHART 5C

BUSINESS CYCLE SERIES: 1948 TO PRESENT—Con.

NBER Leading Indicators—Con.

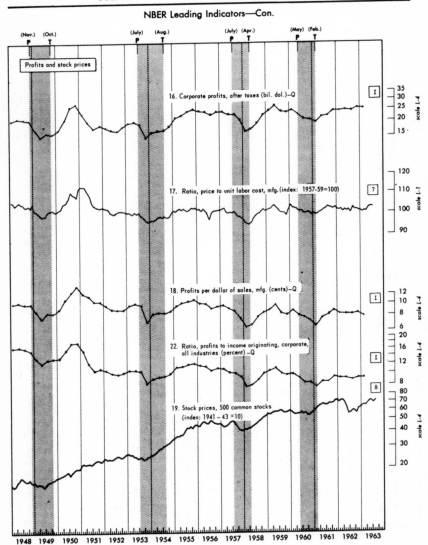

Profits and stock prices

16. Corporate profits, after taxes (bil. dol.)–Q

17. Ratio, price to unit labor cost, mfg. (index: 1957-59=100)

18. Profits per dollar of sales, mfg. (cents)–Q

22. Ratio, profits to income originating, corporate, all industries (percent) –Q

19. Stock prices, 500 common stocks (index: 1941 – 43 =10)

1948 1949 1950 1951 1952 1953 1954 1955 1956 1957 1958 1959 1960 1961 1962 1963

CHART 5D

BUSINESS CYCLE SERIES: 1948 TO PRESENT—Con.

NBER Leading Indicators—Con.

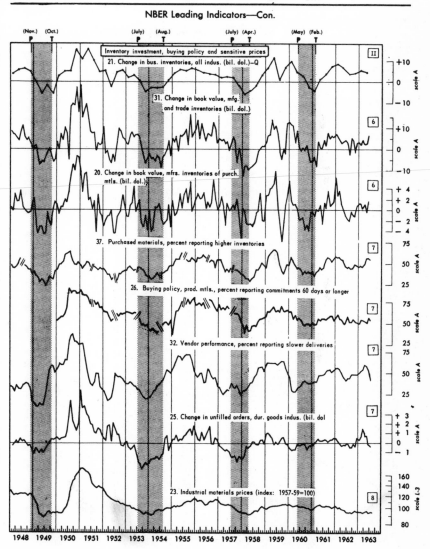

CHART 6

BUSINESS CYCLE SERIES: 1948 TO PRESENT—Con.

NBER Lagging Indicators

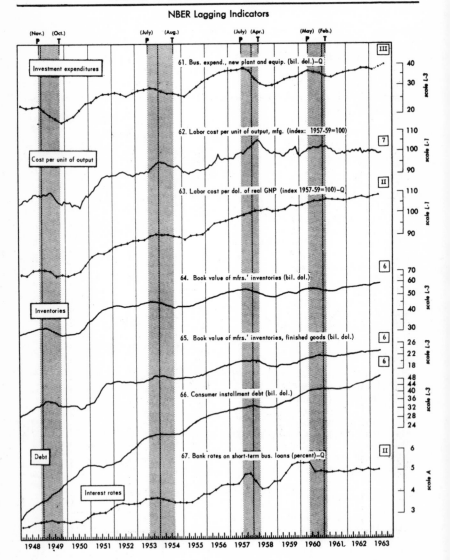

again needed. Also, when reductions in overtime are possible, this will achieve a lower cost per hour than will a commensurate reduction in the work force.

TABLE 10
RECORD OF TIMING OF SELECTED STATISTICAL INDICATORS AT BUSINESS CYCLE TURNS*

— Lead + Lag	PEAKS		TROUGHS	
	Number	Average Lead Months	Number	Average Lead Months
LEADING INDICATORS				
1) Average hours worked	7	− 7	8	−4
2) Accession rate (manufacturing)	9	−10	10	−3½
3) Layoff rate (manufacturing)	9	− 8	9	−5
4) Durable goods new orders	7	− 6	7	−2
5) Housing starts	8	−13½	8	−5
6) Commercial and industrial building awards	7	− 9	7	−1½
7) Net new businesses	20	− 3	22	−5
8) Failure liabilities	17	− 7	18	−7
9) Corporate profits (net)	8	− 4	9	−2
10) Common stock prices	19	− 4	19	−5
11) GNP inventory change	4	−17½	4	−5½
12) Industrial raw materials prices	8	− 7½	9	0
COINCIDENT INDICATORS				
13) Nonagricultural employment	16	0	16	0
14) Unemployment rate	5	− 4	6	+1½
15) Industrial production	17	0	17	−1
16) GNP (current dollars)	6	+ ½	7	−1
17) GNP (1954 dollars)	3	0	3	−3
18) Bank debits outside New York City .	16	+ 1½	17	−3
19) Personal income	8	+ 1	9	−2
20) Retail sales	6	+ 2½	6	− ½
21) Nonfood wholesale prices	6	0	7	+1
LAGGING INDICATORS				
22) Plant and equipment expenditures ..	9	+ 1	9	+2
23) Unit labor cost	6	+ 6½	6	+7
24) Manufacturers inventories	7	+ 1½	7	+3½
25) Instalment credit	4	+ 5½	4	+3½
26) Bank loans interest rate	8	+ 5	9	+5

*Statistical Indicator Associates, North Egremont, Mass.

The Gross Accession or Hiring Rate, Manufacturing

Changes in the hiring rate sensitively reflect the efforts of employers to increase the number of persons they employ. Typically, several months elapse after a downturn in the hiring rate before it is reduced below the separation rate (largely quits and layoffs), and a decline in employment occurs. During this period, the length of the workweek usually declines. Since the hiring of labor is influenced by wage rates and productivity, labor costs per unit of output and profits are particularly useful in analyzing cyclical movements in the hiring rate.

Layoff Rate, Manufacturing

Layoffs are the chief means by which cyclical changes in unemployment occur. Layoffs are closely related to additions to unemployment and to reductions in employment, except when the layoff immediately obtains another job. Cyclical turns in the layoff rate have nearly always preceded cyclical changes in unemployment and the opposite turn in nonagricultural employment.

New Orders, Durable Manufacturing Goods Industries

New orders for durable goods is one of several series that represent investment commitments by businesses. Several studies by the National Bureau of Economic Research have demonstrated that the volume of activity in these early stages of the investment process tends to fluctuate in advance of changes in such broad measures of activity as production, income, and employment. This order series has shown a persistent tendency to lead the production output of the industries receiving the orders, as one might expect. Again, the many factors that contribute to the early declines in orders during business expansions are rising cost-price ratios, tighter money conditions, and the rapid accumulation of inventories. Improvement in the above factors is typically associated with an improvement in the orders trend. The size of order backlogs should be observed in relation to changes in orders, since high backlogs may delay the impact of declining orders, whereas low backlogs may hasten the effect.

Housing Starts

Housing starts are particularly sensitive to such short-range factors as the state of the money market and changes in housing legislation. In addition, such longer-range factors as changes in construction costs, marriage rates, and vacancy rates are influential. Since housing starts represent an early stage in the construction process, they lead such factors as residential construction employment and expenditures, tend to lead production of construction materials and household appliances, and also have an impact on the demand for furniture and other household furnishings. New orders for materials used largely in housing are closely related to starts as are residential mortgage commitments.

Commercial and Industrial Building Contracts

Contracts for construction are also an early stage in the investment commitment, and are affected by changes in costs and profitability as are new orders. These contracts, however, are more closely related to the level of business activity than are housing starts, and appear to be less sensitive with respect to changes in financial markets. Quarterly estimates of new capital appropriations have been available for about a decade and have been closely correlated with commercial and industrial contract awards. Since there is a long period of construction, both series lead plant and equipment expenditures.

Net Change in Number of Operating Businesses

This series includes the number of newly established businesses minus the number discontinued. The number of businesses discontinued is roughly coincident with cyclical change, but the number of new businesses as well as net new businesses leads. As with other factors related to the investment process, the timing of net new businesses is closely associated with changes in profits. Substantial increases in profits and profit margins tends to induce, with a slight lag, the creation of a large number of new businesses. As costs rise and profit increases become less widespread in the advanced stages of the business cycle expansion, the number of new businesses decline. A business contraction reduces new business formation, but before the cycle trough is reached, the number of firms and industries experiencing rising profits increases and induces an increase in new business formations.

Business Failures, Liabilities, Industrial and Commercial

The total number and aggregate liabilities of business failures usually declines as business improves and rises as business deteriorates. The liabilities of business failures usually lead not only business activity but also the number of failures, thereby reflecting a tendency for the failures of large concerns to move ahead of those of smaller concerns. Large failures begin to increase before economic activity turns down as a result of declining profitability in the later stages of the business expansion. Higher labor costs per unit of output, rising inventories, and tighter money conditions probably all contribute to the process. Large business failures continue to rise during the contraction, but usually reach their peak and start declining before the business cycle trough is reached. Lower costs per unit of output and resulting improvement in profit prospects and reduced financial strain probably account for the lead at the trough.

Corporate Profits after Taxes

Since actual and potential profits play a central energizing role in a free market economy, they play an important role in the generation of the business cycle. Profits provide the incentive and funds for investment, they generate business optimism and pessimism, and they encourage business expansion and contraction. Rising costs in the last stages of a business expansion and a slower rate of increase in physical production contribute to an adverse profit trend before the business cycle peak is reached. The opposite forces work during a business decline.

Common Stock Prices

Profits and interest rates are closely associated with the pattern of stock prices in the business cycle. As explained in this book, changes in liquidity and in interest rates tend to alter the desirability of holding stocks, and their prices typically move in advance of the business cycle turning points.

Change in Business Inventories

Changes in business inventories are extremely volatile and account for the bulk of cyclical change during mild business recessions. These changes have shown a persistent tendency to reach cyclical turns before GNP. Inventory changes do not become negative before business cycle peaks, but they tend to become smaller. Likewise, decreases in inventories usually become smaller before troughs in the business cycle. NBER studies indicate that it is the purchased material component of total inventory change that is primarily responsible for the early timing of changes in the total.

Industrial Material Spot Market Prices

This index includes the daily prices of 13 raw materials which sensitively reflect forces affecting open markets and organized exchanges. Attempts to build or pare down materials inventories tend to be reflected promptly in the index. Therefore, changing profitability of business which affects inventory change is reflected in prices paid. These prices also tend to lead business cycle turning points.

STATISTICAL MEASURES AND DATA INTERPRETATION

In observing changes in the above series, several adjustments must be made in order to detect a meaningful change. As is true in analyzing most data, the first elementary step involves the elimination of seasonal movements. Also, in some cases it is necessary to use moving averages to smooth erratic elements in the series. Several summary measures are designed to show how widespread and how fast the movements of cyclical developments are occurring.

When evaluating trends in the indicators, it is desirable to rely on the impression given by the total group rather than to fix attention on only one or a few indicators, since each of the indicators does not work every time. One device for combining data and giving an impression of the pervasiveness of the cyclical movement is called the diffusion index. The diffusion index is a simple scheme for adding up figures and producing a sort of index number. To construct a diffusion index, merely count up in each group the number of items that are rising at a particular point in time, and take this number as a percentage of the total indicators in that group. In other words, a diffusion index represents the per cent of indicators expanding at a given point in time. Such a series will show how widely diffused expansionary or contractionary forces are in the sector under consideration. Even after making seasonal adjustment, using a moving average when necessary and computing diffusion indexes, the series are still erratic sometimes.

It is useful to compute diffusion indexes for each of the leading, coincident, and lagging indicators so that the development in one set may be compared with developments in the other sets. Chart 7 shows that a diffusion index of the leading indicators tends to rise prior to the rise in the index of coincident indicators. The laggers, of course, are the last to reflect a changing business trend.

Diffusion indexes may also be used to show the percentage of companies, industries, or geographic areas which are experiencing rises over the time interval measured. The scope of expansion or contraction usually narrows before peaks and troughs in business cycles are reached, and diffusion indexes measure this phenomenon. Therefore, diffusion indexes are useful predictive devices, because they almost always reach their highs and lows before business cycle peaks and troughs. They also serve to point out the important fact that there is rarely a period when all business activities are moving in the same direction. At all times, cross currents are encountered which complicate the task of the analyst.

After studying a large number of diffusion indexes, Geoffrey H. Moore made the following conclusions regarding their properties and what they reveal about the economy:[5] (1) Cyclical movements in the economy are general, but far from universal. Diffusion indexes seldom show all economic series going in the same direction. (2) There is little evidence that cyclical movements have become either more or less general in recent years. (3) The leads or lags that certain series exhibit to one another are usually reflected in diffusion indexes constructed from the components of the series. (4) The scope of a business cycle expansion diminishes before the peak in total economic activity is reached, and the scope of a contraction diminishes before the trough in total economic activity is reached. (5) Once expansion in the economy has become general, when measured in such a way that cyclical factors are exposed, it stays general for a considerable time. These periods are usually longer than those in which contraction is general. (6) The scope of a contraction shortly after it begins is correlated, though often only loosely, with the severity of the contraction.

---

[5] *Ibid*, pp. 79–86.

CHART 7
DIFFUSION INDEXES

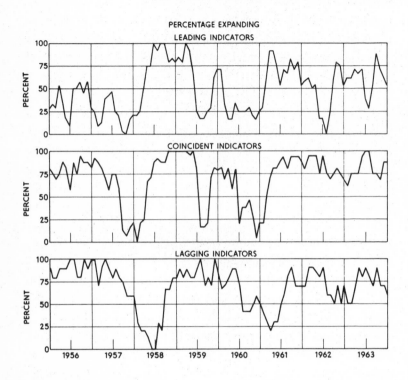

Source: Statistical Indicator Associates, North Egremont, Mass.
Data presented in Appendix B.

Another statistical technique useful in business cycle analysis compares the behavior of the current business cycle phase
with behavior during the corresponding phase of previous business cycles. In each issue of *Business Cycle Developments* there
are comparisons similar to those in Chart 8 which show the
movements of series from previous business cycle peaks,
and comparisons are shown of the movements of series from
their previous cycle low points as in Chart 9. Such data are useful in placing current cyclical movements in proper historical
perspective.

Another useful summary measure represented regularly in *Business Cycle Developments* is referred to as "amplitude adjusted" general indexes. These indexes combine various series measuring different types of economic activity such as production, employment, and prices in a single index. The technique standardizes the month-to-month percentage changes of each series so that all series are expressed in comparable units. *Business Cycle Developments* adjusts each series so that its average month-to-month change, without regard to direction, is one. This approach facilitates an interpretation of the current month's change with respect to earlier periods as well as with other series. The individual amplitude in adjusted series have been weighted and combined into a single index. This index also has been adjusted so that its average month-to-month change is one. This index provides a composite measure of the amplitude and pattern of the business cycle. For example, if the index shows an increase in the current month of 1.5, this means it is rising 50 per cent faster than its average rate of increase in the past; if the increase is only 0.5, it is rising only half as fast as the historical average. This index should be interpreted with knowledge that economic activity tends to rise most rapidly in the early stage of a business cycle expansion and slows as the cycle matures.

It is also possible to compute a composite index for the leading, coincident, and lagging indicators. This index is useful in determining whether the cycle trends in the series are widespread and likely to be cyclical in nature or due to isolated phenomena, such as a strike or the decline in stock prices in May and June, 1962. An example of such indexes appears in Chart 10.

Another useful technique for identifying peaks and troughs of business cycles involves "timing distributions" of current highs or lows showing the number of individual series reaching highs during each of the recent months of an expansion, or lows

CHART 8

COMPARISONS OF REFERENCE CYCLE PATTERNS

Percent of reference peak levels measured from the reference peak date preceding the
trough of each of 4 recent business cycles to 30 months after the trough of each cycle.

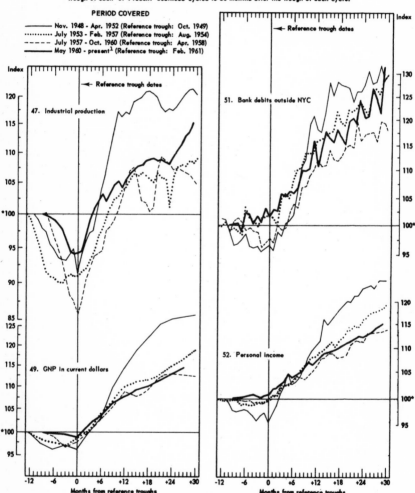

PERIOD COVERED

―――――― Nov. 1948 - Apr. 1952 (Reference trough: Oct. 1949)
·············· July 1953 - Feb. 1957 (Reference trough: Aug. 1954)
――――― July 1957 - Oct. 1960 (Reference trough: Apr. 1958)
―――――― May 1960 - present[1] (Reference trough: Feb. 1961)

47. Industrial production

49. GNP in current dollars

51. Bank debits outside NYC

52. Personal income

Months from reference troughs

*Reference peak level. For series with a "months for cyclical dominance" (MCD) of "1" or "2", the figure for the reference peak is
set at "100". For series with an MCD of "3" or more, the average of the 3 months centered on the reference peak month is set at "100".
For quarterly series, the reference peak quarter is set at "100".

CHART 9

COMPARISONS OF SPECIFIC CYCLE PATTERNS

Percent of specific trough levels of selected series compared for 4 business expansions. Period begins
with the specific trough date of each series for each expansion.

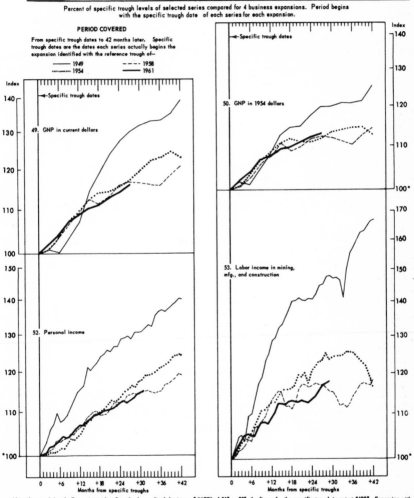

*Specific trough level. For series with a "months for cyclical dominance" (MCD) of "1" or "2", the figure for the specific trough is set at "100". For series with an MCD of "3" or more, the average of the 3 months centered on the specific trough month is set at "100". For quarterly series, the specific trough quarter is set at "100".

during recent months of business contractions. As new highs or
lows are reached, the current highs or lows will be moved
ahead. Comparison of the current timing distributions with
those for periods near earlier business cycle peaks and troughs
are useful in deciding whether recent evidence suggests a turning point is at hand. *Business Cycle Developments* presents
detailed timing distributions each month.

REPETITIVE ASPECTS OF BUSINESS CYCLES

There exists no foolproof method of determining in advance
the length or depth of a recession once it is under way, or the
length and extent of a recovery currently in progress. Nonetheless, the prudent and enterprising observer is not helpless. The
National Bureau of Economic Research has carefully docu-
mented and codified most of the relevant facts concerning the
26 U.S. business cycles since 1854. Knowledge of what usually
happens during a business cycle is of great aid in estimating
what will happen in the current one. Many observers, caught up
in the milieu of the present, are far too prone to assume existing
conditions are unique. Sometimes they are, but usually the
present is merely repeating the past in many significant re-
spects. Since one cannot study the future, it is important to
study and know the past as a guide to interpreting the present.
An organized search for similarities between current economic
trends and the past is likely to be far more fruitful than a search
for existing but frequently insignificant differences. Even to
isolate significant unique differences, the analyst must know
the past. Knowledge of the past can hopefully limit future
mistakes in analysis to at least those pertaining to unique conditions rather than errors in analyzing repeating trends. Furthermore, one's self-respect and confidence are more readily restored following an error based on a new set of circumstances

CHART 10
Composite Indexes

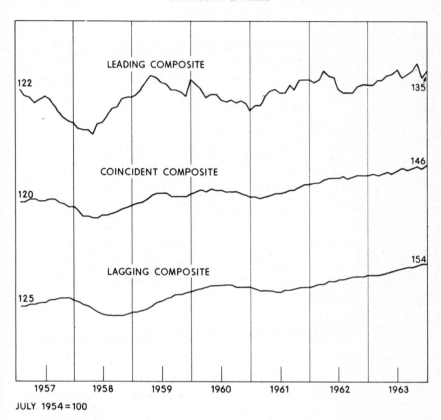

JULY 1954 = 100

Source: Statistical Indicator Associates, North Egremont, Mass.
Data presented in Appendix B.

than an error due to ignorance of history, even though each may be equally costly.

Despite many differences in detail, Geoffrey H. Moore of the NBER has isolated the following significant similarities of past business cycles.[6]

1. Recovery from the lows in output, employment, and

[6] See various essays written by Geoffrey H. Moore in *Business Cycle Indicators*, Vol. I.

profits has usually taken place at a faster pace after severe depressions than after mild contractions.

2. However, the magnitude of a cyclical advance in stock prices typically varies inversely with the severity of the previous business decline. In other words, the market has tended usually, but not always, to react with confidence after a mild recession but with caution after a severe one.

3. Despite a faster economic pace after severe contractions, reattainment of previous peak levels has taken longer because the preceding recession was deeper.

4. Nearly every business expansion has carried total output, employment, and profits beyond the level reached at the previous peak.

5. The rates of advance in total economic activity during expansions have been more uniform throughout the expansion than have been the rates of decline throughout the contraction. Therefore, a more accurate projection of the ultimate rate of advance of a business expansion can be made early in the expansion than can be made of the ultimate rate of decline at the beginning of a contraction. Comparative data of present and previous business expansions are frequently useful in forming a view as to the strength of the current rise.

6. The rate of growth in output, employment, and profits has been consistently larger in the initial stages of a business expansion—the first six to nine months—than in later stages. After the initial phase, slower growth has been the rule, especially after the preceding peak level has been regained.

7. The average length of nonwar business expansions since 1854 has been about 26 months, with only two—other than those occurring during war periods—lasting longer than 37 months. The expansion following the Great Depression of 1929–33 lasted 50 months. Only five expansions out of 26 lasted less than 20 months. During the past 40 years, no recovery has lasted less than 20 months. There has been a general

tendency within the past 40 years for recoveries to last longer and declines to be shorter than previously, with the exception of the long-lived 1929–33 decline and also the abortive 25-month 1958–60 recovery.

8. The weakness in the NBER leading indicators in the early months of a recession is closely correlated with the ultimate severity of the contraction. An experiment performed by Moore in the fall of 1960 suggested that the existing contraction would be milder than all contractions since 1920 except that of 1926–27, which was among the least severe of the previous 25 business cycle contractions in the National Bureau's records dating back to 1854.[7] It is now possible to state that the 1960–61 recession was milder than any downturn since 1920 except the small dip in 1926–27.

Careful analysis of developing economic trends as measured by the leading, coincident, and lagging indicators, in the light of the above long-standing patterns, will greatly improve current economic judgments. It is the thesis of this book that beneficial results will also flow from a continuing analysis of monetary trends which the NBER approach largely ignores.

EVALUATION OF INDICATOR APPROACH

In a broad sense, there can be no reasonable doubt that the indicators when properly presented and adequately analyzed record the tendency of some series to lead business cycle turning points, others to coincide, and the remaining to lag. The indicators also truly reflect the tendency for the scope of business expansions to become more narrow as the business cycle ages and for the scope of contraction to become less as the business trough approaches. Therefore, in hindsight an analyst can usually point with justifiable pride to the fact that indica-

---

[7] Geoffrey H. Moore, statement on the current economic situation before the Joint Economic Committee of the Congress, December 7, 1960.

tors again faithfully recorded classic tendencies inherent in the U.S. business cycle. But the most critical question is: Does the indicator approach enable the analyst to recognize these changes as they are occurring, and can he use this information to predict the next turning point with a high degree of accuracy? The candid answer must be a qualified no, but it should be followed by an equally candid admission that the future can never be known with certainty and that no other forecasting approach has a virtual monopoly on accurate predictions. Perhaps a fairer question might be: Does the indicator approach provide clues which will improve the ability of the careful analyst to anticipate the next turning point? Here the answer must certainly be yes. Since progress toward the solution of important and difficult tasks can seldom be by great leaps forward, a prudent analyst must gratefully accept whatever guidance is available. The results achieved by business analysts in anticipating postwar business cycle swings were usually improved substantially because of the availability of the NBER indicator methodology.

But why is the approach not capable of nearing perfection? A brief review of the inherent limitations would be a prudent exercise.[8] First it should be recognized that the indicators sometimes give what in hindsight proves to be false signals. But, unfortunately, we search for a foresight mechanism. The indicators are sensitive not only to impending major cyclical declines, but also to minor declines as well as periods of leveling out of economic activity. For example, the leaders weakened in 1951, but the economy expanded modestly on net balances as the rise in defense activity more than offset weakness in the private sector. In 1956, the indicators again suggested weakness in the economy, but the recession was delayed until 1957 perhaps due to a large backlog of capital appropriations and a

---

[8] Also see Frank E. Morris, *Business Cycle Indicators*, Vol. I, pp. 110–19.

high level of unfilled orders. Again in 1962 the indicators declined, but the economy merely leveled off and later strengthened. Weaknesses were correctly reflected before each of the
postwar recessions, but sometimes the leaders strengthened
briefly before the downturn as in 1948 and 1960. At all times
it is extremely important to interpret the indicators within the
entire business complex including private trends as well as
government policies and not merely to mechanically apply
the indicator approach.

A second and related difficulty is the tendency for the leaders
to record a variable lead time between cycles. It is to be expected that some leading indicators will tend to have a longer
lead in any particular cycle than other leaders, but that can be
allowed for if the typical leads are well in mind. For example,
housing starts, the accession, and layoff rate typically have
longer leads than do such leaders as new orders and the average
workweek. But, regrettably, there is also considerable variability in the lead of any particular indicator from cycle to cycle.
Sometimes allowance for this variability can be made by reference to such economic factors as the size of backlogs of unfilled
orders and unspent appropriations and the level of unstarted
building contracts, but much of the difficulty of interpretation
inevitably remains.

Also, economic activity may be affected by political and
international developments that are basically noneconomic in
character and usually are not encompassed in the indicator
statistical system but, nevertheless, have important economic
consequences. Modern examples of such developments include
the Korean conflict during the 1949–53 expansion which turned
out to be unusually long, the steel strikes of 1953, 1956, and
1959, and the Suez crisis in 1956. Even the threat of steel
strikes may accelerate inventory accumulation and thus distort
the true economic picture that would otherwise be reflected by
the leaders.

Despite heroic attempts to devise mathematical mehods of processing the data and thereby eliminating irregular and seasonal movements, some erratic movement remains. It is also unfortunately true that the leading series tend to be the most erratic. Therefore, it is most difficult to distinguish between random interruptions of the underlying trend and true cyclical change in the series. To complicate matters more, revisions of the data occur rather frequently. Therefore, the analyst sometimes does not know for sure what has actually happened in the past, practically never knows what is happening at present, and is even less certain of what will happen in the future.

Finally, the leading indicator technique for predicting business cycle fluctuations is not grounded in a cohesive, unifying theory as is the monetary approach developed in this book. Although it is possible to explain why individual indicators react as they do with respect to the business cycle, there exists no unifying explanation. In the absence of such a theoretical foundation, confidence concerning future trends must inevitably be impaired. Nonetheless, past experience suggests that careful analysis of indicator trends will be of aid to the analyst, particularly if used in conjunction with the monetary approach.

To quote an economist and statistician who has done much to improve the indicator approach:

The difficulties of using the indicators are formidable. In interpreting current changes we are sometimes confronted with false signals, pauses in the underlying trend, variability in the performance of our most trusted series, shifts in attitudes arising from external events, and errors of measurement. Progress has slowly, but steadily, been made to reduce these difficulties. . . . However, while the inherent difficulties of forecasting changes in our vast and complicated economy may be reduced, they will never be completely eliminated, so that we shall always have to contend with a margin of error in our forecasts.[9]

---

[9] Julius Shiskin, "Business Cycle Indicators: the Known and the Unknown," *Business Cycle Developments*, September, 1963, pp. 69–79.

The fainthearted and defeatists should never attempt to analyze current business trends for the avowed purpose of attempting to determine the probable future course of economic activity. This task is not and cannot be completely a science, as a large element of judgment will inevitably remain. A wise professor of business forecasting once responded to a student's question as to how he was able to reach a precise quantification of his views about the future state of business: "I am always uncomfortable with any statistical projection of the future. I therefore choose the statistical projection with which I am least uncomfortable and thereby minimize my discomfort." For those interested in minimizing their discomfort concerning the probable future course of the economy, an understanding and application of the indicator approach will be helpful. It provides a useful, even though imperfect, supplement to the monetary approach presented in this book.

VI

Changing Liquidity and the Business Cycle

MONETARY HYPOTHESIS

MONEY PLAYS a minor role in the conventional National Bureau of Economic Research indicator analysis of the causal factors influencing business cycles. Analysts of the U.S. business cycle have learned much from the pioneering efforts of such men as Wesley Claire Mitchell, Arthur F. Burns, and Geoffrey H. Moore, but recent evidence suggests they underrated the impact of monetary change on the business cycle. Before viewing the evidence, let us elaborate the theory that places money in the star role.

The theory which contends that changes in the amount of money is the major factor determining the demand for goods and services is generally called the quantity theory of money. Peculiarly enough, it is not a new theory, but the point of view was sent into nearly total eclipse with the development of the Keynesian theory of income and employment in the mid-1930's. For at least a century and a half, economists have contended that the amount of money in an economic system is an important determinant of total spending and the general price level. Since many prices, including wages, are inflexible downward in the short run, it appears plausible that monetary change may affect short-run employment and production trends. Perhaps the most effective means of approaching an understanding of the quantity theory is by using the "equation of exchange" developed by Irving Fisher during the early part of the twentieth century.[1]

The equation of exchange separates the relevant factors of the economy into four broad categories defined as follows:

M = average quantity of money during a given period.
V = average turnover of money during a given period.
P = average price level of goods and services sold during a given period.
T = volume of transactions during a given period.

If we multiply M, the money stock, times V, the average turnover, we have MV which is the amount of money spent on transactions during the period under consideration. Likewise we can multiply P, the average price level, times T, the unit measurement of volume of transactions, and secure a total PT which represents the amount of money sellers of goods and services received for their sales during the period under consideration. Since the amount of money spent in any period must be equal to the amount of money received, it therefore follows that $MV = PT$. This equation is labeled the equation of exchange. It is clear that the equation of exchange is a truism, correct by definition, and, hence, is not the quantity theory of money. The above equation does not have the basic essential of any useful theory—namely, the capacity for being disproven. Nonetheless, the equation of exchange, $MV = PT$, does serve a useful function by establishing the categories with which the quantity theory is concerned.

---

[1] See Irving Fisher, *The Purchasing Power of Money* (New York: Macmillan Co., 1926).

It is possible to make a useful reformulation of the equation of exchange by substituting X (total real output during a given period) for T. There exists no adequate measure of T, but real output is measured and reported each quarter in the real gross national product series which represents the real value of finally produced goods and services after adjustment for price changes. In the reformulation of the equation of exchange, $MV = PX$, the definition of M remains the same, but V is now defined as the average turnover of money spent on final production during a given period, and P becomes the average price level of finally produced goods and services during a given period. This price series is quantified in the series usually referred to as the GNP price deflator. It is clear that $MV = PX$, since MV now represents the amount of money spent on current production during a given period, and PX represents the amount of money received from the sale of current production of goods and services during the same period.

To convert the "equation of exchange" into the quantity theory, an assumption must be made concerning independency and dependency of the variables contained in the equation. In other words, the equation of exchange says nothing about what variable provides the motivating force. All it says is that a change in any one variable will be affected by sufficient change in one or more of the other three variables so that MV remains equal to PX. All versions of the quantity theory consider M, the quantity of money, to be an independent variable so far as this proposition is concerned, even though, as explained previously, it can be determined by the monetary authority, i.e., the Federal Reserve System. Theorists argue that V, velocity, is determined by both long-term and cyclical factors. It is in this area that much of the debate over the effects of a changing stock of money is centered. Some contend that changes in velocity automatically offset changes in the money stock; therefore, a changing stock of money does not affect prices, output, and, hence, employment. It is not necessary to assume that V is constant in order to derive a useful theory as some extreme versions of the quantity theory imply. It is only necessary that we establish that changes in V do not consistently offset changes in M, so that changes in the money stock do affect total spending.

Quantity theorists argue that the price level is a dependent variable determined by the volume of total spending and the level of output. Potential total output is determined by such long-range factors as the amount of labor and capital available, as well as the productivity of the factors of production. It is clear that actual output is determined also by total spending. After full employment is attained, it is impossible to increase output further except by an increase in either the amount of capital or labor or an increase in their productivity. However, output can be increased when the economy is functioning at less than full employment by increasing total spending. Earlier classical economists once argued that there would be a tendency for an economic system to maintain full employment at all levels of demand, but it is clear that in the real, contemporary world, prices and wage rigidities tend to lead to reduced employment when total demand weakens.

From the above analysis, an economist would predict that a decline in total spending would lead to both lower output and increased unemployment. Furthermore, if we momentarily assume that velocity changes do not compensate for changes in the money stock (this assumption is to be considered later), a quantity theorist would predict that a decline in the rate of monetary growth would shortly result in a recession due to the adverse effect on total spending. A quantity theorist would argue, conversely, a rise in the rate of monetary growth would shortly increase total spending and, hence, would result in recovery in economic activity.

The argument can be made in a somewhat different and

perhaps more meaningful fashion. Economic units, including individuals and businesses, attempt to diversify their holdings of assets between nonmonetary assets such as real estate and monetary assets such as demand deposits and currency. Their willingness to hold money will depend on its cost, i.e., the sacrificed return from not holding other assets and the demand for money for exchange purposes. At any point in time with a given stock of money, economic units either will have an optimum distribution of nonmonetary to monetary assets and projected expenditures or will be attempting to achieve such an optimum. If the stock of money is rapidly increased relative to other assets and projected income, economic units will find they have an excess of money. They therefore increase their spending on assets and goods, and this action will have the effect of bidding up prices if the economy is at or near full employment but will primarily raise output if unemployment exists. This increased spending will continue until prices are bid up to such a level that the decreased real value of assets and expected income will balance the higher stock of money. Conversely, if the money stock is sharply decreased relative to nonmonetary assets and income, economic units will attempt to conserve on cash. Therefore, total spending will decline and thereby exert downward pressure on prices and production to the point where the lower money stock will be in balance with the reduced level of income.

Although economic units cannot actually increase or decrease the money stock through their own actions, since it is determined primarily by the Federal Reserve System, their actions can bring about changes in asset distribution and total spending and, hence, changes in prices and employment.

The above discussion represents the theoretical underpinning which is the basis for the contention that changes in the stock of money affect total economic activity in an understandable and usually predictable fashion.

RELATING MONETARY CHANGE TO THE BUSINESS CYCLE

Neat explanations or rationales are idle intellectual exercises unless they can be verified in the real world. The science of economics may be elegant and challenging to the intellect, but unless it has some relation to the world in which we live and work, it can have little effect on decisions, either private or public. Therefore, it behooves an economist to test the validity of theoretical contentions if they are to be of practical significance.

In the post-World War II period, at least two authors have vigorously contended that the rate of monetary growth influences cyclical changes in business activity—Clark Warburton[2] and Milton Friedman.[3] These two economists have been most responsible for rejuvenating interest in the quantity theory approach. Until recently, seasonally adjusted monthly data on the money stock extending back into the distant past were not available. As a result of a National Bureau of Economic Research project by Professor Friedman and Anna Schwartz, such data are available now. Chart 11 displays changes in the rate of monetary growth from 1918 and a gross national product velocity of money, i.e., current GNP + average stock of money. Unfortunately, the velocity series is available only on an annual basis prior to 1939 but is available quarterly since that time. The time periods from peaks to troughs of business cycles are shaded. (National Bureau of Economic Research datings are used.)

Table 11 relates business cycle turning points since 1919 to turning points in the rate of monetary growth as measured

[2] Clark Warburton, "The Misplaced Emphasis in Contemporary Business Fluctuation Theory," *Journal of Business*, Vol. XIX (1946), pp. 199–220.

[3] Milton Friedman, "The Supply of Money and Changes in Prices and Output," *The Relationship of Prices to Economic Stability and Growth: Compendium of Papers Submitted to Joint Economic Committee* (Washington, D.C.: U.S. Government Printing Office, March 31, 1958), pp. 241–56.

CHART 11
Monetary Growth, Velocity, and Business Fluctuations

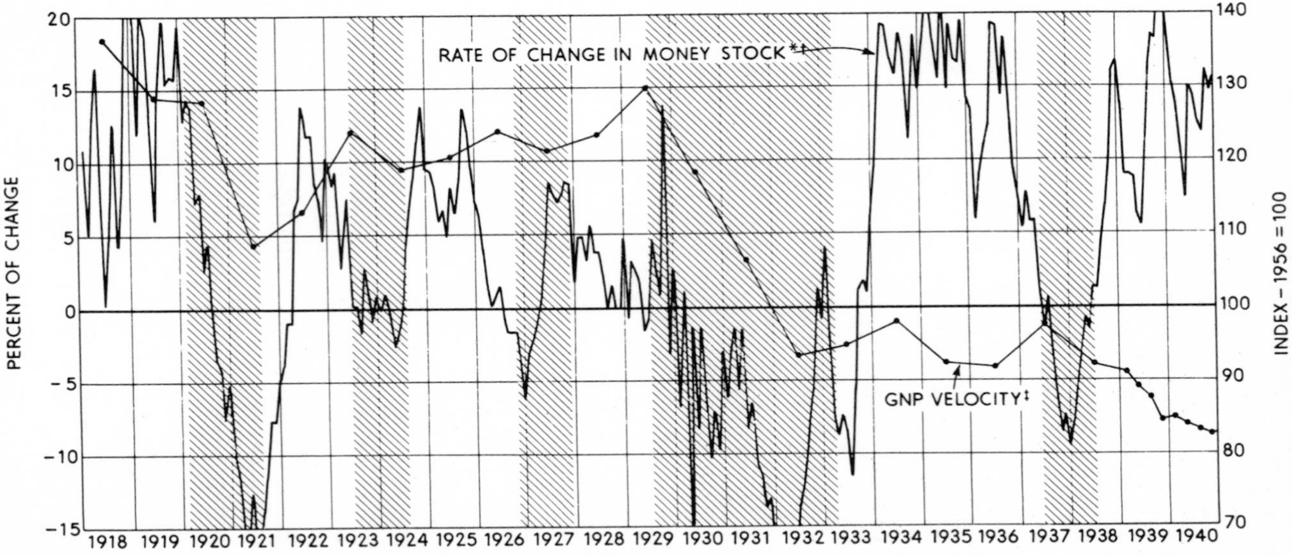

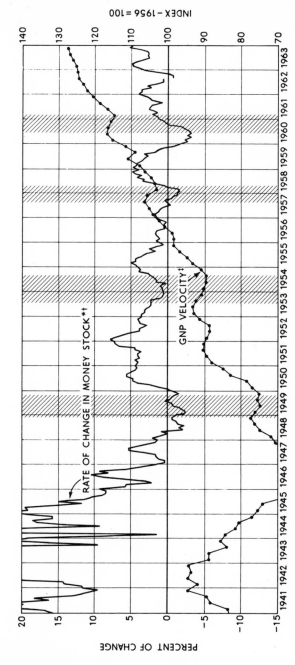

INDEX – 1956 = 100

RATE OF CHANGE IN MONEY STOCK*†

GNP VELOCITY‡

PERCENT OF CHANGE

Source: Department of Commerce, Federal Reserve Board, National Bureau of Economic Research, Inc.
* Demand deposits adjusted + currency (seasonally adjusted).
† Annual rate of monthly change, six-month moving average.
‡ Annual data before 1939; quarterly since 1939.
  Shaded periods are contractions in business activity.
  Rate-of-change data prior to August, 1962, are based on money stock series available prior to modest revisions published in the August, 1962, *Federal Reserve Bulletin*.
  Data presented in Appendixes A and B.

TABLE 11
LEAD OF MONETARY* GROWTH-RATE TURNING
POINTS BEFORE BUSINESS CYCLE TURNING POINTS

		Business Cycle Peaks‡	Months Series Lead		
	Monetary Growth-Rate Peaks†		I	II	III
Series I	Dec., 1918	Jan., 1920	13		
Series II	Dec., 1918			13	
Series III	Oct., 1919				3
Series I	Dec., 1922	May, 1923	5		
Series II	June, 1922			11	
Series III	Jan., 1923				4
Series I	Aug., 1925	Oct., 1926	14		
Series II	Nov., 1924			23	
Series III	Feb., 1925				20
Series I	Jan., 1928	June, 1929	17		
Series II	Oct., 1927			20	
Series III	April, 1928				14
Series I	Aug., 1935	May, 1937	21		
Series II	June, 1935			23	
Series III	Aug., 1935				21
Series I	Nov., 1951	July, 1953	20		
Series II	Jan., 1952			18	
Series III	Dec., 1951				19
Series I	Feb., 1955	July, 1957	29		
Series II	Feb., 1955			29	
Series III	April, 1955				27
Series I	June, 1958	May, 1960	23		
Series II	Nov., 1958			18	
Series III	Mar., 1959				14
			142	155	122
	Range		5-29	11-29	3-27
	Average		17.8	19.4	15.3

		Business Cycle Troughs‡	Months Series Lead		
Monetary Growth-Rate Troughs†			I	II	III
Series I	Jan., 1921	July, 1921	6		
Series II	June, 1921			1	
Series III	Sept., 1921				−2
Series I	Mar., 1923	July, 1924	16		
Series II	April, 1924			3	
Series III	Feb., 1924				5
Series I	Dec., 1926	Nov., 1927	11		
Series II	Dec., 1926			11	
Series III	Dec., 1926				11
Series I	Oct., 1931	March, 1933	17		
Series II	Mar., 1932			12	
Series III	July, 1932				8
Series I	Oct., 1937	June, 1938	8		
Series II	Dec., 1937			6	
Series III	Dec., 1937				6
Series I	Jan., 1949	Oct., 1949	9		
Series II	Feb., 1949			8	
Series III	Jan., 1949				9
Series I	April, 1954	Aug., 1954	4		
Series II	Nov., 1953			9	
Series III	April, 1954				4
Series I	Sept., 1957	April, 1958	7		
Series II	Jan., 1958			3	
Series III	Jan., 1958				3
Series I	May, 1960	Feb., 1961	9		
Series II	May, 1960			9	
Series III	July, 1960				7
			87	62	51
Range			4-17	1-12	−2-11
Average			9.7	6.9	5.7

LEAD BEFORE UPTURNS

°Money stock = demand deposits adjusted + currency (seasonally adjusted).
†Definition of growth-rate series:
    Series I —computed as the per cent change from the preceding month.
    Series II —computed as the six-month moving average of the percentage change from the preceding month plotted on the sixth month.
    Series III—computed as the percent change from the year-ago data.
‡National Bureau of Economic Research datings are used.
Months lead prior to August, 1962, results are based on money stock series available prior to modest revisions published in the August, 1962, *Federal Reserve Bulletin.*

by three methods: (1) Series I computed as the per cent change from the preceding month; (2) Series II, computed as a six-month moving average of the per cent change from the preceding month plotted on the sixth month; and (3) Series III, computed as the per cent change from year-ago data.[4]

The NBER has established a set of useful criteria which denote the characteristics of an ideal statistical indicator of revivals and recessions.[5] (1) The indicator should have a record of perhaps a half-century or longer, thus showing its relation to business cycles in many different conditions. (2) The indicator should lead the month of revival by an invariable interval, and the same should be true for recessions. (3) The indicator should have no erratic movements which serve to mislead the analyst but should have a smooth movement from peak to trough to peak. (4) Cyclical movements of the indicator should be pronounced, so that they can be readily recognized, and should give an indication of the relative amplitude of impending business changes. (5) The indicator should be so related to general business activity that it establishes as much confidence as possible that its future behavior in regard to business cycles will be like its past behavior.

It must be recognized, of course, that in the real world we can never hope to find an ideal indicator, but to the extent that the real world indicators vary from the above criteria, they will be of lesser value to the forecaster. The evidence displayed in Chart 12 and Table 11 accords fairly well with the above criteria. There is a long period of evidence; the series lead both

---

[4] Ideally, it would be desirable to compute a rate-of-change series which is both smooth and sensitive to recent changes in monetary growth. Series I is sensitive but frequently erratic. Series III is smooth, but it is relatively insensitive to recent changes. Series II, which is plotted in Charts 1, 12, and 13, is a compromise series which removes most short-run erratic movements but retains a fair sensitivity to average recent developments. For those reasons, it is probably the best series for present purposes.

[5] Geoffrey H. Moore, *Statistical Indicators of Cyclical Revivals and Recessions* (Occasional Paper No. 31) (New York: National Bureau of Economic Research, Inc., 1950), p. 20.

recessions and recoveries, although not by an invariable inter-val; there are few erratic movements (Series II and III); cyclical movements are pronounced; and the indicator instills confidence, since it is consistent with a well-known and long-lived economic theory. Following are the four important con-clusions that can be derived from these data.[6]

1. All business declines since 1918[7] were preceded by a reduction in the rate of monetary growth. As indicated in Table 11, which presents data covering the last 45 years, the average lead for Series I, excluding the 1945 and 1949 down-turns,[8] has been 17.8 months; the average lead for Series II has been 19.4 months; and the average lead for Series III has been 15.3 months. Since the mid-1920's, the lead of Series II, which is probably the best series, prior to business downturns has varied from 18 to 29 months. The long 29-month lead occurred prior to the 1957 recession when the rate of decline in monetary growth was unusually small.

2. Recoveries since 1918 were consistently preceded by a rise in the rate of monetary growth, with the exception that the slow-moving Series III lagged behind the 1921 business up-turn by two months. As indicated in Table 11, the average lead for Series I has been 9.7 months; the average lead for Series II has been 6.9 months; and for Series III the average lead has been 5.7 months. Since the mid-1920's, the lead of Series II prior to recoveries has varied from 3 to 12 months.

[6] Much of the following material in this chapter appeared in: Beryl W. Sprinkel, "Monetary Growth as a Cyclical Predictor," *Journal of Finance*, Septem-ber. 1959. pp. 333–46.

[7] Other data indicate the same relations existed prior to 1918.

[8] Although 1945 is designated by the National Bureau of Economic Research as a period of cyclical downturn, this cycle was omitted in the above computations because of the nature of the adjustment, which involved primarily a reallocation of resources from production of war goods to production of civilian goods. The rate of monetary growth declined throughout the early postwar period as well as the later years of the war, and it was not until 1949 that a recession developed. Ex-cessive war-created liquidity apparently prevented the usual relationship between a declining monetary growth rate and the business cycle from becoming evident during this period.

For each series, the average lag between a change in the monetary growth rate and the subsequent business change was less prior to recovery than it was before the recession phase of the business cycle. The explanation for this variation is not readily apparent.

3. Typically, the index of GNP velocity of money, which measures the average number of times the money stock is spent on GNP, tends to rise during much of the period when the rate of monetary growth is declining, and tends to decline for a shorter period when monetary growth rises. Indeed, changes in the trend of velocity are approximately coincident with the peaks and troughs of business cycles. This is well known as a result of earlier research.[9] It appears, therefore, that those are correct who contend that countercyclical changes in the money stock are not fully offset by changes in velocity. On the other hand, it is quite clear that there is a tendency during business revivals for velocity to rise in the short run as monetary growth is reduced, thereby softening and delaying the impact of changing monetary growth. Conversely, during a recession as monetary growth begins to rise, velocity continues downward until the trough of the business cycle is reached, again delaying the impact of changing monetary growth for a brief period.

This observation does not mean that changes in monetary growth are useless as a predictive tool, but rather that offsetting changes in velocity merely insert some slippage into the system. Indeed, from a predictive standpoint this is fortunate. The slippage allows time for a lead to be established and, therefore, make possible a prediction based partly on a changing monetary growth rate. If business downturns and upturns coincided precisely with changes in monetary growth, it would,

---

[9] Richard T. Selden, "Monetary Velocity in the United States," in Milton Friedman (ed.), *Studies in the Quantity Theory of Money* (Chicago: University of Chicago Press, 1956), pp. 192–95.

of course, be impossible to use that relationship to predict changes in the business trend unless we could in turn predict changes in the rate of monetary growth.

Even though it is quite clear that velocity changes do not fully offset changes in monetary growth, there remains an interesting question as to why such offsets occur in the short run. The data are consistent with the previous argument given concerning the effect of changes in liquidity on business and consumers. For example, in the early phase of a declining monetary growth period, liquidity is sufficiently high to allow spenders to economize on cash and thereby turn over the existing money stock more intensively. As liquidity is reduced by further declines in monetary growth, this economizing of cash eventually becomes impossible. When this condition is reached, a reallocation of assets and ultimately a change in total spending occurs. The converse appears to be true when monetary growth begins to increase as a recession deepens.

Interest rates probably play a part in encouraging cash economizing as the monetary growth rate declines. Such periods are likely to be characterized by high and rising interest rates. Hence, it is more costly to maintain idle funds, and business is encouraged to economize on cash. Conversely, lower rates during a recession mean it is less costly to maintain idle cash, so an increase in the stock of money may not in the very short run lead to additional spending. Fortunately, from our point of view, it is not necessary to understand this relation completely, since we have a long record which demonstrates that velocity does not for a long period offset changes in growth of the money stock.

4. The evidence indicates that the intensity of changes in the rate of monetary growth is positively correlated with the intensity of subsequent changes in the economy. The most severe recessions or depressions which have been recorded since 1909 occurred in 1920-21, 1929-33, and 1937-38. Also,

the most severe monetary contractions occurred immediately prior to and during those periods. In early post-World War II years, the rate of monetary growth dropped substantially, but the abundance of liquidity prevented a contraction in business. The early post-World War II period represents an exception to the conclusions that business declines shortly follow periods of decline in monetary growth and that large business declines follow large declines in monetary growth. This disparity is readily explained in terms of the economy's expansion in response to the enormous monetary increases during World War II, but it makes clear that a mechanical application of the leading monetary indicator technique and explanation is not justified. Variations in the rate of monetary growth since 1951, when a flexible monetary policy was adopted, have been quite modest in contrast to earlier periods. It is probably not accidental that the economic contractions during that period have also been relatively mild. Finally, the most rapid growth in the money stock following contractions occurred after the 1920-21, 1929-33, and 1937-38 downturns. It is significant that the rates of recovery following those contractions were among the most rapid.

Some recent research by Milton Friedman and David Meiselman of the University of Chicago bears directly on the question concerning the predictive power of monetary change. Their study is entitled "The Relative Stability of Monetary Velocity and the Investment Multiplier in the United States, 1897-1958."[10] In effect, they have attempted to test the relative predictive reliability of the quantity theory, which contends that monetary change is the dominant factor influencing total spending and, hence, income trends; and the Keynesian theory of income determination, which contends that autonomous

---

[10] Milton Friedman and David Meiselman, "The Relative Stability of Monetary Velocity and the Investment Multiplier in the United States, 1897–1958," *Stabilization Policies*, prepared for the Commission on Money and Credit (Englewood Cliffs, N.J.: Prentice-Hall, 1963), pp. 165–268.

investment expenditures are the dominant causal factor. Fortunately, the evidence from their study was remarkably consistent and unambiguous. The income velocity of the circulation of money was consistently and decidedly more stable than the investment multiplied except during the early days of the Great Depression following 1929. Throughout this long period of evidence, there was a close and consistent relation between the stock of money and consumption or income and between year-to-year changes in the stock of money and changes in consumption or income. Furthermore, there was a much weaker and less consistent relation between autonomous expenditures and consumption with the same exception, and essentially no consistent relation between year-to-year changes in autonomous expenditures and consumption. The small relation that exists appears by several statistical tests to reflect the influence of money in disguise.

The correlations between money and consumption were not only higher than between autonomous expenditures and consumption, but they were extremely high in absolute level. For example, from 1897 to 1958 the correlation was .985 between the annual values of the stock of money and consumption outlays, and .695 between the first differences of the series. Correlations between autonomous expenditures and consumption were not only lower than between money and consumption, but they were generally low in absolute level. For the period studied, the correlation was .756 between the annual values of autonomous expenditures and consumption, and .095 between the first differences.

By the application of statistical techniques, the authors attempted to eliminate the effect of money on autonomous expenditures and found that the correlation of autonomous expenditures and income became small and sometimes negative. However, when the identical test was applied to the elimination of autonomous expenditures effects on the money

stock, the correlation between money and consumption remained about the same as with the simple correlation. The
important implication so far as predictive value is concerned
is that the quantity theory approach to forecasting income is
likely to be more fruitful than the income expenditure approach, i.e., the first corresponds to empirical relations that
are far more stable over the course of the business cycle. This
does not mean, however, that the business forecaster should
rely only on monetary change, but it should be a useful supplement to the usual kit of tools.

In a recently published study, *Money and Business Cycles*,[11]
Friedman and Schwartz demonstrated beyond any reasonable
doubt that "the stock of money displays a systematic cyclical
behavior." Furthermore, they concluded that for major movements of income "there is an extremely strong case for the
proposition that sizable changes in the rate of change of the
money stock are a necessary and sufficient condition for sizable
changes in the rate of change of money income." For minor
movements, they concluded that "while the evidence was far
less strong, it is plausible to suppose that changes in the stock
of money played an important, independent role."

Comparisons of monetary and GNP growth for the seven
largest, and largely free market, countries of the free world
also support the contention that monetary change is a prime
determinant of spending change.[12] Those countries with the
more rapid rate of monetary growth in recent years also recorded the largest GNP increase, whereas the United States
which had the slowest growth in the money stock also had the
smallest increase in GNP. The rank correlation between monetary growth and GNP growth for the seven countries considered
was high.

---

[11] Supplement to the February, 1963, issue of *Journal of Economics and Statistics*.

[12] See: Beryl W. Sprinkel, "Relative Economic Growth Rates and Fiscal-
Monetary Policies," *Journal of Political Economy*, April, 1963, pp. 154–59.

WHAT DOES IT ADD UP TO?

The above data and interpretation demonstrate that the monetary evidence is consistent with the hypothesis that monetary changes influence total spending and, hence, cyclical fluctuations. In other words, one would expect, for theoretical reasons, that changes in monetary growth would exert important influences on the trend of the economy, and the data presented are consistent with the hypothesis that monetary changes are causal. More important from our present point of view, changes in the rate of monetary growth have a sufficiently consistent leading relation (not lagging, as some contend) to changes in the business trend to make it a useful predictive tool. This conclusion appears to be warranted, even though one may not be convinced of the causal relationship.

We have not proven that changes in the rate of monetary growth cause changes in business activity. One cannot prove the correctness of any theory in either the physical or social sciences. A careful student can only hope to formulate an internally consistent hypothesis, and then check to see if the facts are consistent with the implications of the hypothesis under consideration. If over a long period of tests the data continue to be consistent, one is increasingly confident that the relationship will continue to exist in future situations. The mere fact that the relation has held in the past does not prove either that the hypothesis is correct or that the relationship will hold for the future. When it becomes clear that a given theory is consistent with observed facts, one should tentatively accept the theory unless later investigations turn up inconsistent observations. The above data justify provisional acceptance of the correctness of the quantity theory of money and, therefore, justify continued reliance on the foregoing relation as a predictive instrument unless someone uncovers a significant contradiction, in which case the hypothesis should be modified or rejected.

There is reason for having confidence in the leading monetary indicator approach, since it is grounded in a well-tested economic theory. It is important to bear in mind that the final test of this and other forecasting techniques must be: "Does it work?" The leading monetary indicator technique appears to fare reasonably well on this score.

VII

Changing Liquidity and the Stock Market

STOCK PRICES AND MONETARY GROWTH— LEADING INDICATORS

BOTH MONETARY change and stock prices lead business cycle turning points, and both series can, therefore, be classified as leading indicators of economic activity. But since monetary changes have a longer lead over business cycle turning points than do stock prices, it follows that monetary change leads stock prices. It was an awareness of these simple leading relationships that was responsible for sparking the investigations, reported in this book, which have turned up additional evidence bearing on the pervasive influence of monetary change.

On the average, the monthly Standard & Poor's index of 425 industrial stock prices has turned downward four months prior to past business cycle peaks. However, not even the stock market has invariably turned ahead of past business cycle peaks. For example, the monthly average peak of the 1927-29 bull market in stocks was reached in September,

1929, whereas the business peak was attained in June 1929. In that exceptional period, stock prices lagged behind the business cycle turning point. In the 1954-57 bull market, stocks hit a double peak as measured by some price indexes —one in July, 1956, and another in July, 1957. The first occurred 12 months prior to the 1957 business cycle peak, somewhat longer than average, whereas the second peak was coincident with the 1957 business peak. Again in 1959, stock prices registered a double peak. The first occurred in July, 1959, 10 months prior to the subsequent business cycle peak, and the second was reached in December, 1959, five months before the business cycle high. But in general in the past 40 years, stock prices turned down prior to the peak in business activity. During the same period, stock prices hit their trough prior to the trough in business activity, with the exception of 1921 when stock prices lagged the business cycle trough by one month. In the 1960-61 recession, stock prices reached a low in October, 1960, four months prior to the business cycle trough.

It must be remembered too that infrequently the stock market experiences a cycle all its own, apparently unrelated to the business cycle. In 1939 and 1940 when war broke out in Europe and for a while went badly for the Allies, the U.S. stock market broke sharply despite strong underlying monetary and economic trends. Again in 1962, the market suffered a sharp break even though a recession did not follow shortly. However, favorable liquidity trends restored most of the losses within several months; and stock prices eventually rose to new highs before liquidity trends became unfavorable.

Knowledge of the facts concerning the usual lead relation between stock price changes and business cycle changes points up the extreme difficulty of attempting to forecast the first from a forecast of the second. Although stock price data are available currently, business data usually become available

one to four months after the facts are generated by the economy. One never knows for certain the current state of the
economy and seldom knows its recent state except in a few
major industries such as steel and autos where weekly data
are generally available. Data revisions complicate the matter
further. Unless one can confidently project the business trend
more than six months beyond the last observed data, assuming that data will not be revised later, it will be impossible
to say what will happen to the stock market price trend.

Yet many analysts base their views of future stock prices
on short-run business forecasts. It is no wonder that these
forecasts seldom detect stock price turning points and usually
are right only when present price trends are continued into
the future. Since the most probable price trend, in the absence
of overwhelming evidence to the contrary, is that prices will
continue in the same direction, it is possible with such forecasts to be right most of the time. However, the misses will
occur at the very time when accuracy is worth a great deal
of money, namely, at the turning points of the stock market.
An economist for a leading investment counseling firm once
stated that his management required only six-month forecasts
of business activity for the purpose of setting their investment outlook. It is painfully clear from the above data that
such forecasts are frequently useless in estimating future
stock price trends at turning points even if the economic projections were correct. In fact, they are likely to be completely
misleading at those points where the direction of stock price
movements is the opposite of the business trend.

It is clear that the usual relation between stock and economic trends is for stock prices to turn down when aggregate
business activity has hit new highs and is still rising. Stock
prices typically continue down until well after the upper turning point of the business cycle has been passed, but turn up
before the business cycle trough. Later, when the business

cycle turns upward, the stock market is usually well off the lows. In fact, stock prices and economic activity typically move in the same direction a little over two-thirds of the time but go in opposite directions nearly one-third of the time, and this is the third that is most interesting, most difficult to predict, and yet potentially most profitable.

An alternative to using the prospective business trend to formulate views on the future stock market trend is expressed by the old market maxim, "sell on good news and buy on bad news." It is clear that cyclical stocks should be sold when basic business news is good and bought when business news is bad. Yet this rule does not tell us at what point during the good news sales should be made nor at what point during bad news stocks should be bought. We must not forget that market and business trends do go in the same direction over two-thirds of the time.

Many attempts have been made to develop systems for forecasting the future of stock prices. Few have proved adequate over a long span of time. Many sage investors contend that it cannot be done on a basis consistent enough to make it a worthwhile part of an investment plan. Yet the quest continues.

Unless one is to adopt a defeatist attitude or rely on long "short-run" business forecasts or on hunches, a stock market forecast must be based on something that occurs *prior to* a change in the trend of stock prices. Some have suggested that the composite of leading indicators developed by the NBER should be used. Yet stock prices themselves are among the most reliable leading indicators. Clearly, it makes little sense to attempt to use stock price changes to forecast stock price changes. Some critics contend that the Dow theory, which is based on past market action, attempts to pull off just that remarkable achievement.

As indicated earlier, changes in the rate of monetary growth have consistently preceded business cycle turning points. Stock prices usually do so. In fact, the average lead of changes in monetary growth prior to the business cycle peak is about 19 months compared to a four-month average lead of stock prices. Changes in monetary growth lead cyclical upturns by an average period of about seven months, whereas stock price upturns occur about five months prior to business upturns on average. Therefore, changes in monetary growth lead changes in stock prices by an average of about 15 months prior to a bear market and by about two months prior to bull markets.

However, the data indicate only the *average* lead of changes in monetary growth prior to a change in stock prices. Although averages may be useful statistical summaries for some purposes, they may be very misleading in other cases. Well known is the story of the gentleman who drowned in attempting to wade across a river that averaged only one foot deep. Analysts must also be interested in the variability of the data. Although there are statistical measures of variability readily available, perhaps the most convincing test of the usefulness of the monetary growth-stock price relationship would be to apply it.

It should also be carefully noted that there is no apparent inherent theoretical reason why the average lead of monetary change over stock price changes should be about 15 months prior to bear markets and about two months prior to bull markets. In the past, leads of 15 months and 2 months appeared to give the best investment results, as indicated below, but the leads might well change in the future. Our present understanding of why liquidity change affects equity prices does not provide the answer. Substantial variation in the future lead time would seriously limit the usefulness of the liquidity aid to timing investment changes. Since we do not fully understand why the leads have been of the duration recorded in the past, we cannot be certain they will be repeated in the future. Even though we cannot be certain of future lead times, both theoretical arguments and empirical evidence strongly suggest that future liquidity changes will provide some useful guidance to future investment timing decisions. Although the tests performed in this book were of a purely mechanical nature for the purpose of avoiding biased hindsight decisions, the evidence suggests that realistic future use of this tool should not be mechanistic but should be used with prudence while also considering other cyclical and investment information.

INDICATED STOCK PURCHASES AND SALES

Chart 12 displays the same monetary growth series as did Chart 1, and, in addition, Standard & Poor's index of 425 industrial stock prices is charted. In order to test the predictive power of the monetary growth series, it was assumed that a bear market in stock prices was predicted 15 months after each peak in monetary growth, and that a bull market was predicted two months after each monetary growth trough was reached. Accordingly, the periods of predicted bear markets are shaded in the chart, and the periods of predicted bull markets are clear. On the base of the chart, the dark bars encompass the months of economic recession as designated by the NBER. If the predictive power of the monetary growth trend had been perfect, stock prices would have declined in all shaded periods and risen in all clear periods. Although the record was not perfect, it is clear that the predicted trend has a close similarity to the actual trend. Seldom were bear market signals given at the exact peak of the market or bull market signals given at the exact trough, but the indications were close. By adopting such an approach in the past, investors would have participated substantially in all major bull markets and would have significantly reduced their losses in most major bear markets.

Although the record was much better than chance, it was not perfect. In three cases, bull market signals were given at a level in the market slightly above the point at which the previous bear market was signaled—in 1924, 1927, and 1954. Therefore, sale of stocks and repurchase at the beginning of the bull market signal would have resulted in a slight loss. Never was a bear market signal given at a level in the market below the immediately preceding bull market signal. During 1939 and 1940, serious market breaks occurred despite a continuing favorable trend in monetary growth. Probably the unfavorable European war developments were responsible, but in any event, this experience made it clear that outside forces can affect equity price trends despite a favorable trend in liquidity. It should be recognized that an investor following monetary growth trends during that period would have retained his investments in equities and would have eventually sold out at much higher prices in 1946.

The World War II period represents a very unusual set of circumstances, and by one interpretation another bull market signal was given at a level in the market above the preceding bear market signal, thereby resulting in loss. Monetary growth was quite high in the early period of the war and began declining in the second quarter of 1943; 15 months later, in July, 1944, a bear market should have begun. Yet, as indicated in Chart 12, monetary growth had been rising for five months by that time. One could argue that the previously given bear market signal for July, 1944, was thereby canceled, and one should have continued holding stocks. If that had been the interpretation, stocks would not have been sold until April, 1946, 15 months after the declining monetary growth trend which began in January, 1945. In that case, the subsequent bull market signal given for April, 1949, would have been at a level in the market well below the previous sell point.

CHART 12

LIQUIDITY CHANGES AND STOCK PRICES

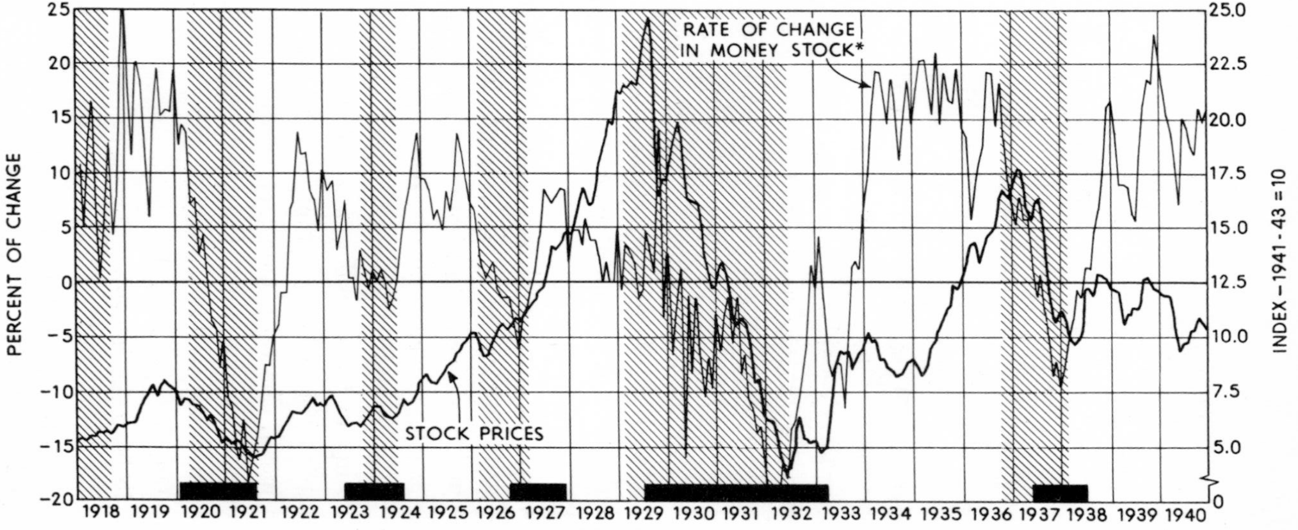

INDEX — 1941-43 = 10

RATE OF CHANGE
IN MONEY STOCK*

STOCK PRICES

PERCENT OF CHANGE

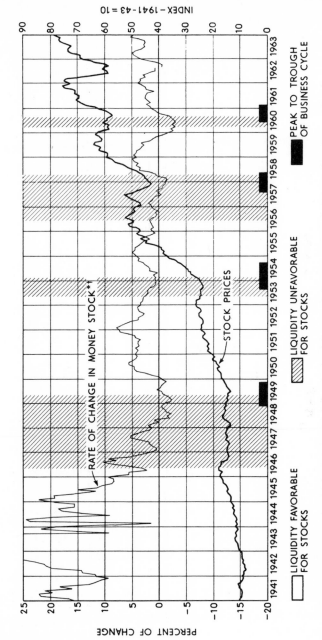

INDEX—1941-43 = 10

RATE OF CHANGE IN MONEY STOCK*†

STOCK PRICES

LIQUIDITY FAVORABLE FOR STOCKS

LIQUIDITY UNFAVORABLE FOR STOCKS

PEAK TO TROUGH OF BUSINESS CYCLE

PERCENT OF CHANGE

Source: Standard & Poor's 425 Stock Industrial Index, National Bureau of Economic Research, Inc., Federal Reserve Board.
* Demand deposits adjusted + currency (seasonally adjusted).
† Annual rate of monthly change, six-month moving average.
Price index scale different on upper and lower charts.
Rate-of-change data for postwar prior to August, 1962, are based on money stock series available prior to modest revisions published in the August, 1962, *Federal Reserve Bulletin*.
Data presented in Appendixes A and B.

TABLE 12
PERFORMANCE ON SALES AND PURCHASES, 1918 TO 1960

| Sell Signal | | Sales | | Stock Market Peak | % Gain from |
Date	S & P's Industrials	Date	S & P's Industrials	% Change Signal to Peak	Stock Purchase to Stock Sale
March, 1920	7.31	Oct., 1919	8.10	9.8%	29.2%
Sept., 1923	6.11	March, 1923	7.40	17.4	33.7
Feb., 1926	10.10	Feb., 1926	10.10	0	56.6
Jan., 1929	21.22	Sept., 1929	24.68	14.0	93.6
Sept., 1936	15.17	March, 1937	17.52	13.4	255.3
April, 1946	18.02	May, 1946	18.06	.2	65.5
April, 1953	24.84	Jan., 1953	26.45	6.1	69.4
May, 1956	49.64	July, 1956	52.27	5.0	94.3
Feb., 1960	59.60	July, 1959	64.23	7.2	32.5

Buy Signal		Stock Market Trough			
Date	S & P's Industrials	Date	S & P's Industrials	% Change Signal to trough	% Loss Avoided from Stock Sale to Stock Purchase
Aug., 1921	4.57	Aug., 1921	4.57	0 %	37.5%
June, 1924	6.45	Oct., 1923	5.99	7.7	(5.6)
Feb., 1927	10.96	April, 1926	9.06	21.0	(8.5)
May, 1932	4.27	June, 1932	3.80	12.4	79.9
Feb, 1938	10.89	May, 1938	9.78	11.3	28.2
April, 1949	14.66	June, 1949	13.69	7.1	18.6
Jan., 1954	25.55	Sept., 1953	23.26	9.8	(2.9)
March, 1958	44.97	Dec., 1957	43.29	3.9	9.4
July, 1960	59.25	Oct., 1960	56.90	4.1	.6
				Average 8.6%	

Further appreciation July, 1960, to February, 1964, 38.3%.

Again in 1962, a sizable market break occurred despite the fact liquidity had not been adverse long enough to suggest market difficulties. The cause of the break may remain enshrouded in doubt, but, clearly, economic and liquidity trends were not the dominant factor influencing investors' desires to held equities. In any event, as indicated in Chart 12, the rising liquidity trend which began in the fall of 1962 preceded the rise in equity prices by about one month. The market recovered its loss and rose to new highs, and the economy did not slip into a recession shortly after the market break as usually occurs. It appears the market break in 1962 bears little kinship to the typically business-cycle-oriented stock break.

Table 12 gives specifics on sales and purchases of stocks from 1918 to 1960 based on monetary change, assuming stocks were sold 15 months after monetary growth peaked, and stocks were bought two months after the monetary trough. Following the 1960 purchase, no sale was indicated through 1963.

Over the test period from 1918 to 1960, bear market signals were given when average prices were within 8.1 percent of stock market peaks, and bull market signals were given within 8.6 percent of stock market troughs. Many investors might be quite satisfied if their records had been as good! Although the above relationship appears reasonably close, there are difficulties in application, to be discussed later, that make a mechanical use of the approach quite hazardous. Nonetheless, when applied with prudence, indications given by the monetary growth trend can be a useful and profitable investment tool.

WHY DO CHANGES IN MONETARY GROWTH AFFECT STOCK PRICES?

There can be no final answer to the question posed above, for the answer must be modified in the light of future experience. Some will contend the relation is spurious and the often observed consistent lead is due to chance and will not be repeated in the future. Such an argument would be more plausible if it were not for the fact that all cyclically related stock price movements, since 1918 at least, have corresponded closely to monetary change. The monetary indicator failed to signal the 1939-40 and 1962 breaks, and neither of these stock price declines appeared to be related to a subsequent business recession. This monetary approach was first developed in mid-1957. The buy indication in early 1958, the sell indication in early 1960, and the buy in 1960 proved to be correct. It failed to warn of the 1962 decline, but improving liquidity that autumn shortly preceded the recovery in stock prices. This experience does not demonstrate that the relation will continue to hold in the future, but it does cast doubt on an assertion that the relation is a fabric of hindsight application and bears no implications for the future. Foresight predictions are a much more severe test of the predictive power of a theory than are hindsight forecasts. By either test, the monetary approach remains reasonably well intact, albeit not completely unscathed.

Some may contend that other factors cause changes in both monetary growth and stock prices, and that changes in the first in no sense "cause" the second to change. This may be true, but it would be more convincing if one could determine what the "other factors" might be. In any event, so long as changes in monetary growth continue to lead stock price changes, one need not be convinced that the relationship is causal. If one were to contend that business conditions bring about both the decline in monetary growth and in stock prices, it is difficult to explain why both series begin declining when business activity is still rising, and why both series begin rising prior to a subsequent upturn in economic activity. Furthermore, it was demonstrated previously that monetary growth is determined primarily by monetary policy actions taken by the Federal Reserve Board rather than by the impact on the banking system of changing business conditions.

If we are to argue that changing monetary growth in some sense causes changes in stock prices, a plausible explanation must be developed. We suggest the following hypothesis.

The causal force is conceivably related to the changing liquidity of the economy relative to the liquidity desires of economic units, including businesses and consumers. The demand of the community for money will grow as incomes rise and interest rates decline, i.e., asset values grow. As incomes rise, the community desires to hold a larger volume of money to accommodate the larger transaction volume. Also, demand for money increases as interest rates decline, for the cost of maintaining idle cash is less. Transaction demand for money increases over the long-term trend of the economy and also during the expansion phase of the business cycle. If monetary growth is reduced at that time by Federal Reserve action, it will become necessary for the community to adjust growing liquidity needs relative to existing liquidity.

As indicated previously, neither individuals nor businesses separately or in aggregate can increase the stock of money in the economy, since in our economic system the basic source of liquidity must be the Federal Reserve System. But separate economic units can attempt to improve their own liquid position. The extent to which one spending unit succeeds in doing so will, however, be at the expense of another. How can an adjustment to changing liquidity be attempted? First, spending units can attempt to conserve on cash balances when liquidity decreases during the expansion phase of the business cycle. There will be an additional incentive to do so during periods of rising economic activity, for interest rates typically rise also. Therefore, it becomes more costly in terms of sacrificed income to hold large cash balances. Such adjustments will tend to increase the velocity or turnover of money.

It has been previously observed that velocity tends to rise during the expansion phase of the business cycle. But as the liquidity squeeze continues relative to liquidity desires, it will become necessary to make additional adjustments. There will be an attempt to shift from less liquid to more liquid assets. This force may be evidenced by fewer purchases of readily marketable assets such as stocks and by a tendency to shift from stock purchases to bond purchases—a more liquid type of asset. Finally, some will convert less liquid assets into cash and near substitutes. There will be an increased volume of stocks offered for sale. In order to entice purchasers, the price will have to decline. Eventually, further attempts at liquidity adjustment through the financial markets will become more difficult and costly, and total spending will be affected adversely. Perhaps the last resort will be an attempt to acquire liquidity by spending less relative to income. When a sizable number of spending units resort to this device, total spending will decline, and the economy will enter a recession. But prior to the recession, stock prices would have declined.

But why the upturn in stock prices at the very time when prospects for employment and earnings are deteriorating? It seems unlikely that investors in the aggregate can properly forecast the subsequent upturn in economic activity when individual professional forecasters have so much difficulty. Again, there may be a basic force operating on investors and the economy for bringing this development about, even though it was not predicted by the investing public.

As incomes and asset values decline, the desire for liquidity on the part of economic units recedes, assuming there is no cumulative crisis of fear or a further liquidity squeeze resulting in a crisis. If at the same time the Federal Reserve encourages growth in the money stock and, consequently, the basic liquidity of the economy, some investors will become willing to give up some of their excess liquidity. For an individual unit, this may be done by ceasing to sell readily marketable, less liquid assets and eventually by buying such assets. There may be a tendency for investors to shift out of liquid assets into less liquid assets. Again, the changing interest rate pattern encourages this shift. Interest rates are typically low, so that the return on fixed-value assets will be lower than previously relative to the dividend yield on stocks. During the declining phase of the economy, some investors will be willing to hold more cash, since interest rates are low. Therefore, velocity will recede. However, as liquidity increases, stock prices are likely to respond by ceasing to decline and eventually by rising, even though the short-run trend in business activity continues to deteriorate.

Let us trace the sequence of events over the business cycle in somewhat more detail. First, assume the economy is in balance in the sense that the amount of money desired by the community is equal to the existing stock and that investors are content with their present diversification of assets. Now, let us suppose that an increased rate of monetary growth occurs in response to open market purchases by the Federal Reserve Open Market Committee.[1]

If the purchase was from a commercial bank, the bank would have excess reserves in place of government securities, and there would be an incentive to rearrange its portfolio, since excessive liquidity would exist. If the purchase was from a nonbank seller, the seller is likely to hold the cash only temporarily but will deposit the check in a commercial bank, thereby adding to banking system excess reserves. Therefore, in either case the liquidity of the banking system would be increased, and in the last case the nonbank seller has a

---

[1] For an elaborate discussion of this adjustment mechanism see: Friedman and Schwartz, "Money and Business Cycles," *Review of Economics & Statistics*, Supplement: February, 1963, pp. 59–63.

higher ratio of money to total assets than was true prior to the sale. In neither case would the seller of government securities be in a position of balance, even though he was willing to sell the securities to the Federal Reserve Open Market Committee at the favorable price offered. There exists an incentive to rearrange investment portfolios by exchanging cash for a less liquid asset. The commercial banking system will in the process of using its excess reserves increase total assets and also the stock of money.

It seems reasonable to expect that both the nonbank and bank holders of redundant balances will attempt first to purchase securities comparable to those just sold, i.e., fixed interest securities which entail low risk. But in the process of buying these securities, prices will be bid up, and buyers who now have excess cash will search farther along the investment spectrum. Banks may then attempt to expand loans, and other investors may add to other higher risk, fixed-coupon obligations and, eventually, equities, real property, etc.

As the process of monetary expansion and asset adjustment develops, the initial impacts are diffused throughout the economy in several ways: (1) The rank of assets affected widens. (2) Creators or builders of assets find that the price of assets has been increased, and it becomes profitable to step up the rate of production. This rise in asset value would encourage business enterprises to increase capital expansion, while demand for homes, an important nonfinancial effect, would encourage home building, and demand for consumer durable goods would tend to raise production of these items, and so on. Therefore, it is apparent that the initially redundant cash balances concentrated in the hands of those first affected by the open market purchases triggered a series of responses throughout the economy.

It can be readily seen that the monetary stimulus is spread from the financial markets to the markets for currently produced goods and services. As the prices of financial assets are bid up, they become expensive relative to nonfinancial assets, so there is an incentive for investors to adjust their total portfolios of assets by acquiring nonfinancial assets. As the prices of existing nonfinancial assets rise, they become expensive relative to newly constructed nonfinancial assets. The rise in the prices of nonfinancial assets tends to encourage the direct purchase of current assets services rather than the purchase of the assets. This tends to raise the demand for current productive services both for producing new capital goods and for purchasing current services.

The foregoing explanation is quite consistent with many of the observed regularities of the business cycle, including the pattern of security price changes. The rate of growth of the money supply is usually increased by the Federal Reserve System early in a business contraction. Recalling the explanation above, we would expect the first impact of increased monetary growth to be reflected first in financial markets. The attempt to restore holdings of fixed-coupon securities would result first in a rise in bond prices. Later, as investors adjusted farther out the investment spectrum, equity prices should rise, and finally, as nonfinancial asset prices were bid up, the flow of payments for goods and services should increase. That is the pattern found in the typical business contraction. The above sequence of events transmitted from a Federal Reserve open market purchase explains why bond prices typically move ahead of stock prices which, in turn, rise before the trough in the business cycle occurs which coincides with the increase in production of goods and services. It is important to recognize that the Federal Reserve and the commercial banking system play a central role in the transmission mechanism that results in the cyclical fluctuations of the bond and stock markets. Monetary contraction would have the opposite effects on the financial markets and production recited above.

The central element in the transmission mechanism is the banking system which initiates balance sheet adjustments throughout the economy as investors attempt to adjust their actual stocks to their desired stocks. In this stock-flow explanation, money is a stock in a portfolio of assets, similar to the stock of financial assets or nonfinancial assets such as houses or buildings or inventories. It yields a flow of services like other assets. It is subject to change by action of the Federal Reserve System, and in the view expressed above, this change is the central motivating force resulting in business cycle disturbances and the related fluctuations in stock prices.

As asserted previously, there is no way of proving the above explanation is the correct one. But it is consistent with the observed relation of economic and stock price trends over the business cycle. Until a contradiction is discovered and a superior explanation is offered, the above rationale should be provisionally accepted. Although it is comforting to our intellect to be able to explain seemingly contradictory developments, this cannot be a valid test of the theory that changes in monetary growth affect stock prices in a predictable way. The only acceptable test is one of predictive power. To put it in the words of the nickname of one state—Show Me. Based on predictive power, the monetary theory of stock price fluctuation appears to fare well even though not perfectly.

PITFALLS IN APPLICATION

The foregoing test established that there is an observable and, to a large extent, predictable relation between changes in the rate of monetary growth (liquidity) and changes in the prices of industrial stocks. A rationale based on an expanded version of the quantity theory of money appears to "explain" the relationship. Although it is possible to apply this relation to investment policy, there are many difficulties in addition to possible future changes in lead times that should be recognized in order to avoid dangerous pitfalls. It should be recognized that peaks and troughs in monetary growth were selected in hindsight and that favorable and unfavorable liquidity periods for stock prices were accordingly determined by those selections. Hindsight selection is always easier than foresight decision-making. It requires little knowledge and judgment to be an excellent Sunday morning quarterback. Nonetheless, it is reasonable to believe that a careful analysis of monetary theory and policy can within a narrow range of error select critical liquidity turning points at the times they occur. Since the monetary-stock price relation was developed in 1957, there have been three opportunities to test abilities to select turning points in monetary growth at the times they occurred. In each case, it was relatively easy to make the proper identification, even though the decisions were not without accompanying doubts and concerns. Once again, it should be pointed out that a monetary approach will not detect the infrequent fluctuations in stock prices which are unrelated to underlying business cycle phenomenon.

It is relatively easy to determine bear market signals with a high overall accuracy because of the long lead between the change in trend of monetary growth and the subsequent action point. The previous test was based on a bear market signal following the peak in monetary growth by 15 months. In fact, one could have chosen any period within the range of 12 to fifteen months with approximately equal results. This means that the observer has at least a year in which to make up his mind as to whether there has or has not been a change in the monetary growth trend if past patterns are repeated. If the basic liquidity trend continues down for one year or longer, investment policy should be based on the assumption that the stock market is near its peak. Conversely, if a downward trend in monetary growth is interrupted by a protracted upward trend before 12 to 15 months have elapsed, the bear market signal should probably be considered canceled before it became effective. This has never occurred except during World War II and 1962.

The major difficulty in application lies in the determination of the trough in the rate of monetary growth shortly before a bull market action point is designated. This problem is a serious one due to the short lead time between the liquidity trough and the bull market signal—only two or three months if past patterns continue to prevail. Since current data on the stock of money lag two weeks or more, the problem becomes even more acute. Sometimes it may be necessary to allow more than a two-month rise in monetary growth before reaching an action point. However, somewhat superior results would have occurred in the past if only a one- or two-month lag had been permitted.

There were many occasions in the past, as indicated in Chart 13, when monetary growth turned up for a period of two or three months and later declined to new lows. Obviously, the careful analyst must utilize additional information in order to form a confident judgment as to whether a recent reversal in a long-time monetary growth decline will be a lasting one. It is here that knowledge of our monetary system, economic theory, current monetary policy, and current economic conditions is crucial.

Since the adoption of a flexible monetary policy in 1951, the Federal Reserve has rather consistently pursued a restrictive monetary policy during periods of rising economic activity and an easy policy during periods of declining production and employment. But the above statement is somewhat oversimplified. The Federal Reserve has been understandably reluctant to base monetary policy on projections of economic soothsayers. But since monetary expansion began on the first month of the business contraction during the 1960-61 reces-

sion, it would appear that economic projections on that oc-
casion played a crucial role. This conclusion is particularly
evident when it is recognized that several expansive policy
actions were taken prior to June, 1960, and also that data
available then did not reflect an existing business downturn.
The timing of monetary expansion with respect to the beginning of the recession was unprecedented in recent times.
Perhaps future policy will be based on economic projections.
If so, it may become increasingly difficult to anticipate a
monetary policy change, since the pattern of the past may
be further disrupted.

Second, during the recovery following the 1960-61 recession, monetary policy remained expansive although somewhat
erratic for a longer period than during previous postwar recoveries. This change was due presumably to concern about
the persisting high level of unemployment of labor and capital resources, even though economic activity was expanding.
An additional factor that perhaps encouraged the change
was the widespread view among economists that the prompt
and substantial shift toward monetary restriction during recovery from the 1957-58 recession was a major factor in
preventing a satisfactory recovery.

However, persistent balance-of-payments difficulties undoubtedly acted as a restraining force on the level of monetary expansion following the 1960-61 recession and also
inserted an erratic element in the rate of expansion.

As indicated in Chart 2, total reserves of member banks
adjusted for seasonal and reserve requirement changes were
moderately down from January through September, 1962, in
sharp contrast to the considerable expansion which occurred
from mid-1960 until early 1962. In other words, the Federal
Reserve aggressively provided additional reserves to the banking system in the earlier period and pursued a policy of
moderate monetary contraction from January through Sep-

tember of 1962. In the last quarter of the year, expansion of bank reserves was substantial. Chart 2 shows that required reserves moved up sharply as more reserves were provided to the banking system, and those reserves were used to expand loans and investments and, consequently, the money stock. As additional reserves became available, expansion in private demand deposits occurred. It appears that additional reserves were provided in the latter part of the year due to the upward seasonal pressure on the bill rate. As bill rates edged upward, it was possible for the Federal Reserve to step up reserve creation and still maintain the bill rate at the level monetary-fiscal authorities felt was consistent with the balance-of-payments restraints.

It should be clear that despite the many years of experience with monetary policy, the art of central banking continues to develop, so monetary experience of the past may not be a perfect guide to the future.

Federal Reserve policy-makers appear to consider a restrictive policy to be one of declining free reserves (excess reserves minus borrowings) and an easy policy one of rising free reserves. However, recently increased attention has been given to adjusted total reserves. For the reasons indicated in Chapter 4, there is a considerable lag between a change in economic policy as defined by changing free reserves and a reversal in the monetary growth trend. The length of this lag will be determined largely by such factors as the rapidity of change in the economy and the aggressiveness with which the Federal Reserve moves. During a period of change from a restrictive to an easy policy, the less the decline in economic activity and the more aggressively the Federal Reserve supplies additional reserves to the banking system, the shorter will be the lag. If the change in policy moves slowly and/or the downward movement in business activity is substantial and fast, the lag will be considerable. Careful analysis of monetary growth and changes in adjusted total bank reserves will be of great aid in determining when an apparent policy change becomes effective. Furthermore, the analyst must be constantly on guard against the possibility that a significant change in monetary growth will occur, even though free reserves remain essentially constant.

In analyzing monetary policy during recessions, the careful observer must seek to determine whether or not Federal Reserve action is more than offsetting other factors tending to reduce monetary growth and how rapidly this action is being taken. Perhaps the first place to look is the trend in free reserves; however, that is not enough. It is possible for free reserves to rise due to a liquidation in demand deposits which reduces the money stock and thereby converts required reserves into excess reserves. If this occurred, there would be, of course, adverse effects on the money stock, even though free reserves were rising.

A more likely development is a rise in free reserves due to a reduction in borrowings by commercial banks from the Federal Reserve. Although this action tends to restore the liquidity of the banking system and in some conditions increases its willingness to expand total assets in coming months, nonetheless, the repayment of debt to the Federal Reserve reduces the sources of potential bank reserves, as explained in Chapter II, and thereby tends to reduce total bank reserves and promote monetary contraction. Therefore, it is important to determine whether or not the Federal Reserve is more than restoring those reserves either by open market purchases or a reduction in reserve requirements which reduces required reserves and thus raises excess reserves. Also, it is important to determine if a rapid gold outflow is occurring and whether the Federal Reserve is more than offsetting this adverse monetary factor. In addition, it is possible that nonreserve uses of potential reserve funds might increase sharply, so that unless the Federal Reserve acted to offset, reserves of banks and monetary growth would be retarded. Therefore, it is particularly desirable in such a period to watch the trend in adjusted total reserves of member banks which reflects all these factors to see that they are rising more than seasonally.

Of course, one cannot be certain that the Federal Reserve will continue a policy of ease once it has begun. However, if business conditions continue to deteriorate, it is very likely that such action will be continued until the recessionary trends are reversed. There have been periods in the past when the Federal Reserve allowed vast liquidation in the stock of money without taking significant counteraction. Although that experience could be repeated, it appears very unlikely that such will occur in the present state of knowledge and political sentiment. Our government is now devoted to the principle of attempting to maintain high levels of employment as stated in the Employment Act of 1946.

Although the mandate to promote price stability is far less clear than the statutory requirement to maintain high employment, the Federal Reserve as a matter of policy has also pursued that objective. Consumer prices typically continue to rise in the early phase of most recessions, and, therefore, these twin objectives come into conflict. Since 1951, this apparent dilemma has been resolved by the Federal Reserve Board in favor of fighting rising unemployment after the Board is definitely convinced that a recession is under way. Since there is a lag in the acquisition of information and since Federal Reserve moves require committee actions, counterrecessionary actions have developed sometimes only with a lag.

Gold outflows during recession periods, when U.S. interest rates became relatively unfavorable, have become in recent years an added deterrent to the continuation of an expansive monetary policy. The Federal Reserve has refused to permit arguments from gold standard adherents to promote monetary contraction during recession periods when gold outflows were large. But this was not always the case. In 1931 during the Great Depression, a rapid gold outflow brought a restrictive monetary policy. Higher interest rates halted the gold outflow, but the resulting vast monetary liquidation undoubtedly deepened and prolonged the business contraction. The nation's monetary policy is usually determined primarily by domestic economic conditions rather than by gold flows as was the case during the gold standard period. Nevertheless, a careful analyst must recognize that conditions change. During recent years, gold flows have become a more important determinant of monetary policy as the deficit in the balance of payments persists.

Identifying a restrictive monetary policy and, hence, an unfavorable climate for industrial stocks is less difficult, but it is not without hazard. Considerable monetary restriction is necessary before stock prices are affected adversely. Therefore, the informed observer has a long period in which to form a judgment. However, it is conceivable that following a long period of restriction, monetary expansion might be adopted before previous adverse liquidity trends unfavorably affected stock prices. It is, therefore, necessary that a careful and continuing analysis of monetary change be carried out at all stages of the business cycle.

In making an informed judgment, the analyst must give attention to the rapidity of deterioration or improvement in the economy. Although the early moving leading indicators will be useful in determining whether or not a downturn or an upturn is a near-term probability, seasonally adjusted coincident indicators such as employment and unemployment, industrial production, and bank debits outside New York City are probably most useful in deciding whether a downturn or upturn is actually in progress. It is particularly important that these and other data be analyzed on a seasonally adjusted basis rather than from the point of view of recent trends in unadjusted data or current data in comparison to a year ago. Only the trend in current seasonally adjusted data can reveal recent developments. The alert analyst wants to know whether economic activity has weakened or strengthened more than usual in recent weeks and months, and is not interested in whether the economy is still above a year ago or whether some seasonal improvement or deterioration has occurred. Frequent reference to business cyclical indicators as reported monthly in *Business Cycle Developments* will minimize danger from those potential sources.

As can be detected from the above analysis, the decision as to whether a new upward movement in monetary growth is occurring and will continue is not an easy one. In the final analysis, a decision to take a more aggressive action on stock purchases based on monetary analysis must be primarily a feeling for conditions rather than a scientific conclusion that now is the time to act. This statement is not meant to deprecate the art of decision-making based partly on solid economic judgment and scientific analysis. But it does mean that every relevant factor must be considered, and the final judgment must represent a mental synthesis of many factors.

Even then, the decision can be only a tentative one, particularly in the early weeks of an aggressive investment policy. This may mean the prudent solution would be to distribute new stock purchases over the two- to four-month period following what appears to be a new expansive trend in monetary growth. Such an action policy would not usually be a serious handicap, since stock prices frequently, but not always, form a fairly wide bottom before resuming a marked upward trend. Since investors always operate in a world of uncertainty, a hedge against the wrong decision is advisable. However, as the degree of uncertainty about an expansive monetary trend subsides, the investor should be more willing to make additional equity investments. On the other hand, if an apparent renewed monetary expansion becomes abortive, additional equity investments should cease. The same reasoning may be applied to reduction of equity holdings following a prolonged contraction in monetary growth. In other words, even if the investor is convinced that changing monetary trends exercise a pervasive influence on stock price trends, plenty of room remains for the exercise of judgment with respect to the speed of executing investment changes. The distribution of stock purchases on sales over time can be related to the investor's view as to the degree of uncertainty concerning continuation of the present monetary growth trend.

A careful and informed analysis of current economic and monetary policy trends is, nevertheless, likely to give an indication clear enough to enable an investor to profit from the changing monetary trend. It should be emphasized, if it is not already apparent, that the monetary growth-stock price relation under discussion is not a strict mechanistic approach but calls for careful analysis of economic and monetary trends by an informed analyst. Suffice it to say that the necessary knowledge and judgment is not readily attained, but then most worthwhile accomplishments are difficult. If it were otherwise, we would all be happy, successful, and lazy!

VIII

Application to
Investment Policy

TIMING—ONLY ONE OF SEVERAL INVESTMENT HAZARDS

SOME MAY say the liquidity approach to timing investment in stocks cannot be considered an aid to formulating investment policy but that it is, rather, a speculative tool. If by speculative the critic means that from time to time a view is formed as to whether the most likely trend in the market is up or down, then the observation is correct. However, some may consider the formation of a point of view on the direction of the market to be more applauded than criticized. For refusal to face up to this issue is to ignore one of the important potential hazards to successful investing. Unfortunately, complete disregard of a hazard does not make it go away. An imperfect solution may well be better than no solution at all. The liquidity aid to timing stock commitments is based on careful analysis of past data and attempts to analyze current developments in the light of long-lasting relations that have been subjected to extensive tests. It is difficult to believe that a relation that has persisted through most periods for a half-century covering periods of prosperity and depression, war and peace, rapid economic growth and stagnation, highly developed commercial and central banking systems and rudimentary financial systems will not hold most of the time in coming years. Furthermore, as previously stressed, the results of this study are consistent with the long-lived and well-tested quantity theory of money.

It must be noted candidly that severe stock price fluctuations have been less prevalent in the post-World War II period; hence, any investment timing technique has been less useful than previously. If we finally reach the millennium when all business cycles are eliminated, perhaps no attention need be devoted to the problem of timing equity investments. Furthermore, if we could be absolutely certain that all future recessions would be mild, the potential gains from successful investment timing actions would probably be minor. Since stock prices have trended upward throughout most of the past fifteen years, a buy-and-hold policy would have been almost as good as timing purchases and sales of equity securities by changing liquidity trends. But nothing was lost by basing action on liquidity trends, and much would have been gained if one of the postwar recessions had developed into a sizable decline. In a sense, a proper application of the liquidity timing device may be looked on as partial insurance against cyclical risk. If the economy and stock markets become even less volatile in the future, application of the liquidity principle is unlikely to prove costly. On the other hand, if a serious business and stock market decline were to develop in the future for reasons not evident at present, the liquidity approach would probably prove valuable. So long as liquidity trends remain favorable, the investor's confidence in the future trend in equity prices should be strengthened. Conversely, a deteriorating liquidity trend should help to alert the investor that equity prices may decline. In summary, even in a world of apparent increasing stability, a careful analysis of monetary trends should at a minimum strengthen confidence in investment decisions as well as provide some insurance against being lulled into what might prove to be a false sense of security.

Although many investors say they make no attempt to forecast stock price trends, their actions frequently belie their words. Any reasoned decision, including the decision to do nothing, must be based on some estimate as to what the future holds. Therefore, candid admission of a point of view, which can be subjected to explicit analysis and testing, is more prudent than avowals of "no opinion" when in fact the investor is acting as if a carefully formed opinion existed. In other words, when a viewpoint is explicitly developed, the resulting decision is likely to be more carefully considered than if an implicit seat-of-the-pants view is permitted to affect the investment decision-making process. An explicit forecast can be tested; hence, new results can be added to present knowledge.

The manner in which the liquidity approach is adapted to a personal or institutional investment policy should vary with the objectives of the investor. Those placing most emphasis on maximum long-run capital appreciation might want to be more bold in applying the principle than those who are interested primarily in steady income and moderate capital gains. It should be recognized that aggressive application of this approach would have in the past avoided most bear markets and would, therefore, have contributed to the preservation of principal. However, income would have fluctuated significantly, even though excellent long-term growth in income would have occurred. It is believed that the liquidity theory can be adapted in some degree to all types of investment programs, be they institutional or personal, defensive or aggressive.

The liquidity approach has some implications for security selection, but the usual problem of choosing the proper security based on investment objectives remains formidable. One objective of investors using the liquidity theory for timing stock purchases and sales should be to hold stocks most likely to do best during bull markets. Stocks which do best in bull markets may not be the same stocks which do best over the entire business cycle or best over the longer pull. For example, a cyclically volatile stock with only average long-term growth performance may be converted into a rapidly growing investment medium if the investor holds the stock only during the upward market phase. Therefore, successful application of the liquidity timing theory may tend to reduce the relative attraction of "growth" stocks over "cyclical" stocks, assuming, of course, that business activity and stock prices continue to fluctuate in both directions. This observation appears even more possible when the dividend yield differential is taken into consideration. Perhaps the type of equities most ideally suited for shift over the price cycle is growth stocks that are also cyclically sensitive. Diversification requirements will perhaps dictate a balance in the portfolio between aggressive and defensive equities in many investment programs, so that prudence must be exercised in emphasizing cyclically sensitive stocks. Regardless of the makeup of the portfolio, the liquidity theory directs investor attention toward reducing holdings of stocks whose prices are particularly sensitive during periods generally unfavorable to equity prices and it encourages stock commitments when monetary growth is expanding.

Observation of how management of investment funds based upon liquidity changes as a guide to timing decisions would have fared in the past cannot provide assurance that similar results will hold in the future. However, unless such an approach has worked reasonably well in the past, there can be no confidence in future performance. Therefore, in this chapter several hindsight investment tests are developed, and results are compared. There are many ways in which the liquidity timing principle may be adapted as an aid to making investment timing decisions. Several of the many possible adaptations are discussed, and past investment results are presented for each. In order to compare these results with other means of making investment timing decisions, investment test results are presented for some of the better-known investment "formula" timing plans. In making hindsight comparisons, it is important that judgment be eliminated as a source of potential bias. Therefore, the tests conducted appear highly mechanistic and largely devoid of the very ingredient that makes some investors more successful than others— seasoned judgment. Although mechanistic abstractions from reality are necessary in order to generate fair and meaningful comparative data, there is no intention to create the impression that such a limited approach to investment management is considered desirable or recommended. Successful investment management requires a judicious application of all the tested knowledge of the financial analyst and the economist and more too. Timing of investment commitments is only one of several basic problems facing the investor, and the liquidity approach developed and tested in this book is only one of several possible techniques available. However, on both theoretical and practical grounds the liquidity approach appears to be a significant step forward from reliance on either formula timing plans or ad hoc reasoning.

All the tests discussed in this chapter assume that the stocks in the account performed as would the Standard & Poor's index of 425 industrial stocks and that all fixed-value funds, unless otherwise specified, performed as did the Standard & Poor's index of long-term bonds. Yet, an investor does not buy the averages. He must buy a particular group of issues. To the extent that a large fund is involved, it is, of course, possible to get sufficient diversification so that the results of the averages may be approximated. A smaller investment fund will be subject to the vicissitudes of the particular stocks held. It should be recognized that the widely used stock averages such as the Dow-Jones and Standard & Poor's indexes do not represent a list of randomly selected stocks. Typically, they consist of a list of common stocks strongly weighted by large, well-seasoned, and generally high-grade issues. Therefore, it is not too surprising that many stock portfolios do not do better than the standard averages. However, it should always be the objective of an investor to achieve better than average results, if not in capital gains then in income or stability or whatever else the investor considers as his major investment objective. To do otherwise would be to admit that the choice of particular securities is merely a matter of chance and that careful analysis, which leads to superior results on average, is impossible. This may be the case, but if it is true, many investment advisers and managers are spending a lot of money needlessly and are making false and misleading claims to their clients. To the extent that the investor can select securities that perform better than the averages, the overall results should be superior to the results discussed below.

APPLICATION TO STABLE INVESTMENT FUNDS

It is convenient to illustrate the application of the liquidity stock timing theory separately for stable and growing investment funds, even though the principles are the same. The tests that are discussed concentrate on overall capital results without allowance for brokerage fees or capital gains taxes. However, a consideration of capital gains taxes and brokerage fees and the effects on investment decisions will be developed later. If the investment plans discussed appear too mechanical, it is due to explicit assumptions which made the tests possible. In actual practice, judgment can and should be applied in solving the investment timing problem.

The most simple and aggressive application of the liquidity

timing plan is made by assuming that during predicted bull market periods all investment funds are maintained in stocks and that during all predicted bear market periods all investment funds are maintained in bonds. In the test of this plan, it was assumed that a $100,000 investment fund was placed in stocks in August, 1918, and no new funds were added since that time. Changes were made as indicated by the changing monetary growth pattern through nine stock price cycles ending in February, 1960. The monetary approach properly indicated an aggressive stock position in summer, 1960, but since the last cycle is not yet completed, results since February, 1960, were excluded, even though there was a further appreciation of 41.3 per cent through February, 1964. This plan is labeled the 100–100 variable ratio delayed adjustment fund (100–100 VRDA). The investment ratio, therefore, varied from 100 per cent stocks and 0 per cent bonds to 0 per cent stocks and 100 per cent bonds. All funds were invested in stocks until monetary growth had declined 15 months, and then all funds were invested in bonds until monetary growth had risen two months. These leads were selected by testing several combinations of leads. Leads of monetary growth change of from 12 to 15 months prior to stock sales and from one to three months prior to stock purchases gave substantially similar results.

In February, 1960, the value of the total investment fund had grown to $11,958,622, and the average annual compound rate of growth in the fund was 12.2 per cent. This return included only capital appreciation and did not count dividend and interest income which might have added 4 to 5 per cent per year. It was, therefore, assumed that all income was paid out and not reinvested in the fund. For the postwar period— April, 1949, through February, 1960—the average annual compound rate of growth was somewhat higher—14.0 per cent. Table 13 presents detailed information on the shifts.

TABLE 13
INVESTMENT RESULTS, 100-100 VRDA FUND

STOCK PURCHASE, BOND SALE DATE	STOCK SALE, BOND PURCHASE DATE	VALUE OF FUND	% GAIN IN FUND FROM STOCK PURCHASE DATE TO STOCK SALE DATE	POTENTIAL LOSS AVOIDED (OR GAIN MISSED) BY REDUCING STOCKS VS. HOLDING STOCKS	
				Percent	Dollars
Aug., 1918		$ 100,000			
	March, 1920	129,200	29.2%	95.9%	$ 46,765
Aug., 1921		128,541			
	Sept., 1923	171,859	33.7	(57.2)	(5,472)
June, 1924		175,949			
	Feb., 1926	275,536	56.6	(79.6)	(18,665)
Feb., 1927		280,330			
	Jan., 1929	542,719	93.6	88.1	382,074
May, 1932		491,269			
	Sept., 1936	1,745,479	255.3	103.5	509,924
Feb., 1938		1,762,934			
	April, 1946	2,917,162	65.5	81.1	440,900
April, 1949		2,814,128			
	April, 1953	4,768,258	69.4	(9.2)	(12,493)
Jan., 1954		4,892,042			
	May, 1956	9,504,504	94.3	46.2	412,876
March, 1958		9,023,196			
	Feb., 1960	11,958,622	32.5		

If instead of switching from 100 per cent stocks to 100 per cent bonds back to 100 per cent stocks, the switch had been from 100 per cent stocks back to 100 per cent cash (100–0 VRDA), results would have improved moderately. In other words, bond investments on average resulted in capital loss. Yields on high-grade bonds have tended to be coincident with cyclical peaks and troughs in postwar years and frequently lagged cyclical turning points in earlier periods. Since the shift into bonds was typically made prior to the business cycle peak, a further rise in yield reduced capital values. Also, bonds were typically sold before the business cycle low and, therefore, before bond price peaks. In February, 1960, the value of the 100–0 variable ratio fund was $13,433,424, and the annual compound rate of growth in the original $100,000 fund was 12.5 per cent. Investment results are given in Table 14.

TABLE 14
INVESTMENT RESULTS, 100-0 VRDA FUND

STOCK PURCHASE, CASH LIQUIDATION DATE	STOCK SALE, CASH ACQUISITION DATE	VALUE OF FUND	% GAIN IN FUND FROM STOCK PURCHASE DATE TO STOCK SALE DATE	POTENTIAL LOSS AVOIDED (OR GAIN MISSED) BY REDUCING STOCKS VS. HOLDING STOCKS	
				Percent	Dollars
Aug., 1918		$ 100,000			
	March, 1920	129,200	29.2%	37.5%	$ 48,424
Aug., 1921		129,200			
	Sept., 1923	172,740	33.7	(5.3)	(9,611)
June, 1924		172,740			
	Feb., 1926	270,511	56.6	(7.8)	(23,031)
Feb., 1927		270,511			
	Jan., 1929	523,710	93.6	79.9	418,340
May, 1932		523,710			
	Sept., 1936	1,860,742	255.3	28.2	524,990
Feb., 1938		1,860,742			
	April, 1946	3,079,008	65.5	18.6	574,112
April, 1949		3,079,008			
	April, 1953	5,217,071	69.4	(2.8)	(149,105)
Jan., 1954		5,217,071			
	May, 1956	10,135,985	94.3	9.4	953,593
March, 1958		10,135,985			
	Feb., 1960	13,433,424	32.5		

The comparative compound rate of growth in the postwar period increased only modestly over the 100–100 VRDA fund from 14.0 per cent to 14.3 per cent as bond yield changes more nearly coincided with business cycle turning points.

It is revealing to compare these results with an all-stock buy-and-hold fund which does not rely on a timing device but merely rides up and down with the general market. For the entire period, 1918 to February, 1960, the $100,000 original investment appreciated to only $1,057,350 for an average annual compound rate of growth amounting to 5.8 per cent. From that date until February, 1964, there was a further appreciation of 36.5 per cent. Therefore, the compound rate of growth for each of the two variable ratio funds was more than twice as great as the all-stock buy-and-hold fund, and the 100–100 ratio fund in February, 1960, was $10,901,272 greater, whereas the 100–0 fund was $12,376,074 larger. Once again the power of compound interest is demonstrated! For the postwar period, 1949–60, the annual growth rate for the all-stock fund was 13.6 per cent, only slightly less than occurred in the variable ratio funds. Of course, if stock prices go in only one direction, namely up, as has been the case in most of the postwar period, it is very difficult to beat an all-stock investment fund. Those investors expecting an uninterrupted upward movement in stock prices in the future should give no further attention to timing stock purchases and sales—just stay fully invested in equities.

Although it would be useful and perhaps revealing to compare the results of timing stock purchases and sales according to liquidity changes with results actually obtained by astute investors, unfortunately, the necessary data are not available. Therefore, comparisons must be made with explicit plans that have been devised and used successfully by a wide range of investors. It appears probable that few investors currently rely exclusively on a mechanistic "formula" type of investment timing plan, but a sizable literature has developed on this subject, and the approach provides a convenient yardstick for comparative purposes. All formula-type investment timing plans attempt to sell stocks when prices are rising and buy stocks when prices are declining. In contrast with the liquidity approach to timing investment decisions, formula timing plans attempt to elminate forecasts of the direction of any given price movement, but they attempt to take advantage of the price fluctuations that do develop. All formula-plan approaches do, however, make some forecast of long-term market behavior if nothing more than the prediction that stock prices will continue to fluctuate in both directions. Some of the more complicated formula timing plans attempt to provide an answer as to whether stocks are currently "too high" or "too low." The liquidity approach to timing stock commitments provides no answer to whether stocks are over- or undervalued in some intrinsic sense, but does suggest the most probable direction of the next major stock price movement.

The initial impetus for formula-type investment plans developed in the years following the Great Depression when it appeared that the economy was performing in a completely unpredictable fashion unrelated to earlier patterns. In more recent years as the economy and the financial markets developed signs of increased stability, formula timing plans became less popular. One of the first attempts to present the philosophy underlying the formula-timing-plan approach as well as some of the empirical results of the various plans was written over two decades ago.[1] Two other well-known books on this subject have been published subsequently.[2] One type of formula timing plan which provides a convenient comparison with the liquidity approach is labeled the constant-ratio plan. There are several variants of the constant-ratio approach. The actual stock-bond ratio chosen by the investor as the basic ratio would depend on such investment objectives as the amount of risk which could be assumed and the yield sought. After choosing the desired stock-bond ratio—50–50, for example—the investor must decide on the method to be used for determining buying and selling action for the purpose of restoring the basic ratio. Adjustments in the stock-bond ratio may be made by such guides as: (1) Stocks may be sold and bonds bought in a like quantity whenever the value of the stock component

---

[1] H. G. Carpenter, *Investment Timing by Formula Plans* (New York: Harper & Bros., 1943).

[2] Lucile Tomlinson, *Successful Investing Formulas* (Barron's Publishing Co., Inc., 1947); C. Sidney Cottle and W. Tate Whitman, *Investment Timing: The Formula Plan Approach* (New York: McGraw-Hill Book Co., Inc., 1953).

of the fund rises a given percentage amount. The reverse action may occur whenever the value of stocks has declined a given percentage amount. (2) Adjustment of the stock-bond ratio may occur whenever a given movement occurs in a particular stock index. (3) The stock-bond ratio may be adjusted so as to bring the ratio back to the basic position initially chosen whenever a given time interval has elapsed.

Perhaps the simplest constant-ratio formula timing device is the 50–50 constant ratio annual adjustment (50–50 CRAA) plan.[3] This approach involves the sale of stocks in those years when the stock market has advanced and the purchase of stocks in those years when stock prices have declined. The adjustment is made once each year on a specified calendar date to bring the equity fixed-value ratio of the total fund back to 50–50. A 50–50 CRAA fund operating from a $100,000 investment in December, 1918, to liquidation in February, 1960, would have appreciated to $452,210 and would have developed a 3.7 per cent compound average annual rate of growth. From February, 1960, until February, 1964, another 21.0 per cent appreciation occurred. For the 1949–60 period only, the compound average annual rate of growth amounted to 5.9 per cent. This fund had the poorest record of all those tested because of several factors: (1) Typically, stocks were sold too soon during a bull market, since an uptrend usually lasts considerably longer than one year. (2) Also, of course, only 50 per cent of the total invested funds benefited from the rise in any event. (3) In periods of significant stock price weakness, 50 per cent of the fund was adversely affected. (4) In the prolonged bear market from 1929 to 1932, additions were made to stocks long before the bottom was reached in stock prices. Usually, however, premature additions did not seriously affect the value of the fund, since most bear markets usually have a rather short life.

---

[3] *Ibid.*, pp. 34-35

A slight variant on this plan performed significantly better than the 50–50 CRAA approach. The only change was to delay the adjustment back to a 50–50 ratio until the bear and bull market indications were given by the monetary growth trend. In other words, the fund began with a 50–50 ratio as before, but instead of adjusting annually, the adjustment was deferred until the appropriate buy or sell indication was given. Sufficient stocks were sold to cut the ratio back to 50–50 if a sell signal was given, but if the signal was to buy, sufficient stocks were purchased to bring the ratio up to 50–50. Over the entire period from 1918 to February, 1960, that fund appreciated from $100,000 to $677,916, thereby reflecting an average annual compound rate of growth of 4.7 per cent. For the postwar period, 1949–60, the annual rate of appreciation improved to 6.5 per cent which was about 10 per cent better than

TABLE 15
INVESTMENT RESULTS, 50-50 CRDA FUND

STOCK PURCHASE, BOND SALE DATE	STOCK SALE BOND PURCHASE DATE	VALUE OF FUND	% GAIN IN FUND FROM STOCK PURCHASE DATE TO STOCK SALE DATE	POTENTIAL LOSS AVOIDED (OR GAIN MISSED) BY REDUCING STOCKS VS. HOLDING STOCKS	
				Percent	Dollars
Aug., 1918		$100,000			
	March, 1920	112,000	12.0%		
Aug., 1921		90,714		12.9%	$ 3,162
	Sept., 1923	110,889	22.2		
June, 1924		115,314		(0.8)	(36)
	Feb., 1926	150,269	30.3		
Feb., 1927		157,963		(12.8)	(1,130)
	Jan., 1929	234,068	48.2		
May, 1932		129,463		21.5	28,709
	Sept., 1936	316,712	144.6		
Feb., 1938		273,639		33.6	21,817
	April, 1946	379,566	38.7		
April, 1949		337,476		11.6	5,544
	April, 1953	442,714	31.2		
Jan., 1954		454,787		(1.4)	(167)
	May, 1956	661,531	45.5		
March, 1958		613,662		9.2	4,848
	Feb., 1960	677,916	10.5		

the CRAA plan. A further appreciation of 20.6 per cent had occurred by February, 1964. This plan is called the 50–50 constant ratio delayed adjustment fund (50–50 CRDA). The improved results stemmed from the delayed sale of stocks based on liquidity or monetary changes during bull markets until the peak was approximated and the delay of stock purchases in bear markets until most of the total decline had occurred. Investment results are recorded in Table 15.

A further variation of the above plan reflected much greater benefits. It is labeled the 60–40 variable ratio delayed action (60–40 VRDA) fund. Under this approach, the fund began with $60,000 stocks and $40,000 bonds in 1918, but when the sell signal was given in 1920 and subsequent years, sufficient stocks were sold to bring the stock-bond ratio down to 40–60. In other words, in all predicted bull markets 60 per cent of total invested funds were initially placed in stocks, and in all predicted bear markets only 40 per cent of the total invested fund initially remained in stocks. From the beginning $100,000 investment in 1918, this fund had appreciated by February, 1960, to $1,275,622 with an average annual compound growth rate of 6.3 per cent. By February, 1964, a further appreciation of 24.6 per cent had occurred. In the 1949–60 period, the average annual compound growth rate amounted to a thumping 8.2 per cent. It is interesting to note that the long-run results of this program were moderately better than the all-stock buy-and-hold fund, and the fluctuation in the value of the total capital in the account was much less. Table 16 records investment results.

The significant improvement recorded by this fund was due not only to the delay in adjustment of the prevailing ratios, but also to the fact that during the beginning periods of bull markets, 60 per cent of the total fund was invested in stocks, and during the beginning phase of the predicted bear market, the fund participation in stocks was sharply reduced to 40

TABLE 16
INVESTMENT RESULTS, 60-40 VRDA FUND

Stock Purchase, Bond Sale Date	Stock Sale Bond Purchase Date	Value of Fund	% Gain in Fund from Stock Purchase Date to Stock Sale Date	Potential Loss Avoided (or Gain Missed) by Reducing Stocks vs. Holding Stocks	
				Percent	Dollars
Aug., 1918		$ 100,000			
	March, 1920	115,440	15.4%		
Aug., 1921		97,771		39.6%	$11,574
	Sept., 1923	121,756	24.5		
June, 1924		126,222		(17.2)	(929)
	Feb., 1926	170,702	35.2		
Feb., 1927		178,288		(31.1)	(3,419)
	Jan., 1929	278,230	56.1		
May, 1932		173,482		39.2	67,440
	Sept., 1936	462,794	166.8		
Feb., 1938		413,368		52.2	53,989
	April, 1946	595,509	44.1		
April, 1949		538,474		31.3	26,027
	April, 1953	747,591	38.8		
Jan., 1954		767,782		(3.1)	(649)
	May, 1956	1,191,402	55.2		
March, 1958		1,110,368		18.3	18,178
	Feb., 1960	1,275,622	14.9		

per cent. As will be illustrated later, maximum stock participation in the fund was frequently well above 60 per cent in the latter phase of bull markets, and the stock percentage was frequently well below 40 per cent near the end of bear markets.

The following table summarizes the pertinent statistical results of the foregoing stable fund tests. All funds began with $100,000, and no new funds were added.

Chart 13 compares total capital appreciation of the various stable funds, and Chart 14 shows the annual improvement in growth rates. Both relate data to the 50–50 CRAA plan.

It appears from the above results that use of a delaying rule based on buy-sell indications as given by the changing trend

TABLE 17
INVESTMENT TEST RESULTS—STABLE FUNDS
(Original Investment—$100,000)

	AUGUST, 1918-FEBRUARY, 1960		APRIL, 1949-FEBRUARY, 1960
	Final Value (Millions of $)	Average Annual Compound Rate of Growth	Average Annual Rate of Growth
50-50 CRAA	.45	3.7%	5.9%
50-50 CRDA	.68	4.7	6.5
60-40 VRDA	1.28	6.3	8.2
100-100 VRDA	11.96	12.2	14.0
100-0 VRDA	13.43	12.5	14.3
All-Stock Fund (Buy & Hold).	1.06	5.8	13.6

in monetary growth significantly improves investment results as compared to either an all-stock buy-and-hold fund or a 50–50 CRAA fund. Although a simple delaying rule appended to the 50–50 CRAA plan yields noticeable improvements, the greatest benefits result from variation in the stock-bond ratios between buy and sell points. It is quite clear from the above results that the greatest gains accrue from variation between 100–0 ratios and that the smaller the variation, the less the gain.

Additional studies indicate that variation in the ratios between buy and sell points maximizes both capital gains and income but also increases volatility. Fluctuation in income was particularly great in the period of low interest rates and high stock yields when a shift from 100 per cent stocks to 100 per cent bonds resulted in a substantial drop in income of the investor, and the reverse shift resulted in a sharp increase in income. Since bond and stock yields have been more nearly comparable in the past decade, shifts between bonds and stocks result in less income volatility.

CHART 13
Comparison of Total Capital Appreciation—Stable Funds

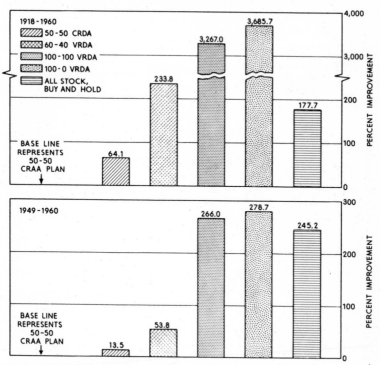

It should be pointed out too that application of the delaying rule substantially reduces the number of trading transactions relative to the number of transactions under an annual adjustment program. For example, under the annual adjustment program covering a period of 42 years, 42 adjustments were made, whereas under the 50–50 CRDA approach, only 15 shifts were made, therefore averaging about one shift every three years. Of course, the amount of purchases and sales at each transaction was considerably larger under the delayed action program, because the per cent of the total funds shifted was greater and the fund was considerably larger, particularly in the later years.

CHART 14
ANNUAL IMPROVEMENT IN GROWTH RATES—STABLE FUNDS

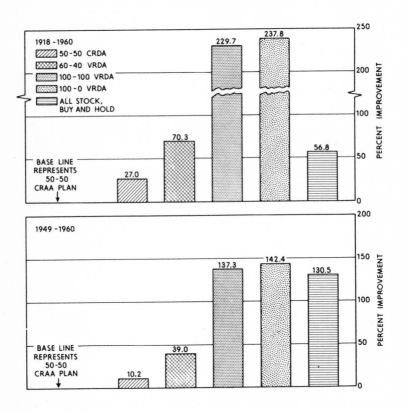

As indicated in Chart 15, there were considerable differences in volatility of the capital values of the various funds over the 42-year period. Fund values are shown only at shift dates, as indicated in the chart. Note that the most volatile fund was the all-stock buy-and-hold fund, and the least volatile fund was the 100–0 VRDA fund. The other funds reflect a degree of volatility between those extremes depending on the per cent of the total fund that was in stocks. It is interesting to note that the 50–50 CRAA fund reflects the greatest volatility of the three remaining funds.

Chart 16 indicates the maximum and minimum stock percentages of the 50–50 CRAA, 50–50 CRDA, and 60–40 VRDA at the adjustment dates. The application of the delayed-action technique results in larger maximum and smaller minimum stock percentages than the constant-ratio fund, since gains are permitted to continue running until near the peak, and losses are reduced in declining markets by a delay in the addition of stocks until stock prices approach their lows. The addition of the variable-ratio technique also accentuated the maximum and minimum stock percentages, because a larger

CHART 15
MARKET VALUE OF STABLE FUNDS

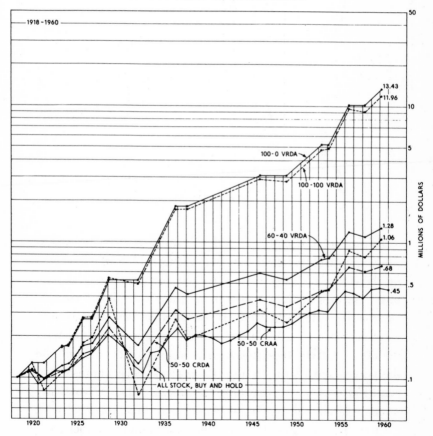

per cent of the total fund was in stocks at the beginning of
bull markets and a smaller percentage was in stocks at the
beginning of bear markets. Since stocks have been less volatile
on average in the past 20 years as compared to the previous
23 years, the extent of both maximum and minimum stock
percentages was less than in the earlier period.

CHART 16
MAXIMUM AND MINIMUM STOCK RATIOS—STABLE FUNDS

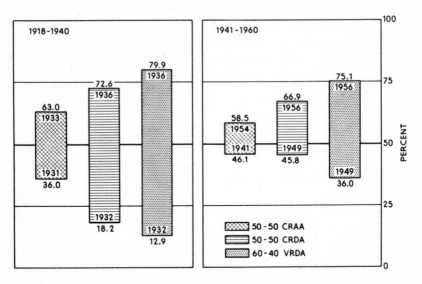

Review of the buy and sell schedules under the various
plans points up the weakness in the CRAA plan which adjusts
by the calendar. Sales occur too early in a rising market, and
purchases are made too soon in protracted declining markets
such as from 1929 to 1932. In fact, 48 per cent of the shifts
were correct in hindsight, and 52 per cent were wrong. With
the 50–50 CRDA fund, total shifts were sharply reduced and
the percentage of correct adjustments was increased to 83 per
cent. Perhaps most important, the misses were only slightly
wrong. It should again be noted that this approach did

not detect the noncyclically related stock market breaks in 1939–40 and 1962. The two shifts in the mid-1920's and the one in 1954 resulted in purchases slightly above the previous sale points. Analysis of the buy and sell schedule for the 60–40 VRDA fund shows that 83 per cent of the shifts were correct and 17 per cent wrong. Again, three sales were wrong in the sense that subsequent purchases were made at a modestly higher level. Total shifts with this fund amounted to 18 compared to only 15 in the CRDA plan, although the number of investment decisions—18—was the same. Differences in the number of shifts in the two plans were due to the fact that no additions to stocks were called for under the CRDA plan when purchases were made above the previous sales prices, but in the VRDA, more stocks were added because the percentages were not up to 60 per cent, even though the previous sale was in error.

APPLICATION TO GROWING INVESTMENT FUNDS

Although there are no new basic principles involved in the application of the liquidity approach to investment of growing funds, the investment problem is somewhat different. Not only is the investor concerned with the management of an existing fund, but also periodic new additions must be invested. In the tests that follow, the existing funds were handled in the same fashion as were the stable funds. Investment of new funds raises some new questions that require resolution. The convention adopted in the following tests was to invest all new money in the same percentage of stocks as the percentage in the existing investments. This convention represents a simple approach but is probably not the optimum solution. It would improve overall results if all new funds were invested in bonds when the bear market signal prevailed, and all new funds were placed in stocks when the bull market signal was flashing. It would, of course, be possible to take a compromise position between these two extremes. It might be prudent to reduce the percentage of new funds committed to stocks as it appears the upward trend in stocks is approaching an end. The amount of improvement in investment results from adopting the second convention would depend substantially on the size of incremental investments relative to the total capital fund.

TABLE 18
INVESTMENT TEST RESULTS—GROWING FUNDS
($100,000 Invested annually)

| | AUGUST, 1918-FEBRUARY, 1960 | | APRIL, 1949-FEBRUARY, 1960 |
	Average Annual Compound Rate of Growth	Final Values (Millions of $)	Average Annual Compound Rate of Growth
50-50 CRAA.........	3.9%	10.33	5.3%
50-50 CRDA.........	4.8	12.86	5.7
60-40 VRDA	6.4	20.08	7.3
100-100 VRDA	11.8	94.28	13.5
100-0 VRDA	12.2	105.29	13.7

The overall results of the tests performed are given in Table 18 and Charts 17 and 18. All tests assumed an original fund of $100,000, with a $100,000 addition each year. Therefore, total investments of new money amounted to $4.2 million. The growth rates count only the appreciation of invested capital and not the annual additions.

Again, the 100–0 VRDA and 100–100 VRDA funds experienced the best overall results, with the 100–0 (12.2 per cent) doing slightly better than the 100–100 (11.8 per cent) over the entire period. In the postwar years, 1949–60, the relative performance of the five funds tested remained the same as for the longer period, but the absolute performance of each was improved. All growing funds incorporating the delaying rule based on changes in the monetary growth rate performed significantly better than the 50–50 CRAA fund which was adjusted on each annual anniversary date. Although the long-term compound growth rate for the 100–0 VRDA fund (12.2 per cent) was only slightly more than three times as large as for the 50–50 CRAA fund (3.9 per cent), the final 1960 value for the first fund was $105.29 million compared to $10.33 million for the second—more than ten times as large. Compound interest again worked its miracles!

In conclusion, it should once more be pointed out that the foregoing tests were based on highly rigid and somewhat

CHART 17
COMPARISON OF TOTAL CAPITAL APPRECIATION—GROWING FUNDS

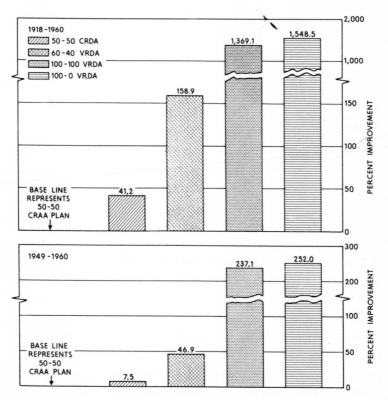

CHART 18
MARKET VALUE OF GROWING FUNDS
$100,000 INVESTED ANNUALLY

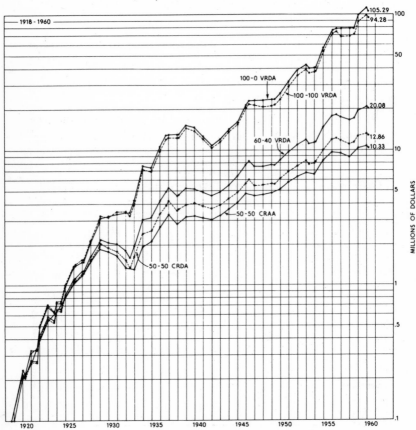

mechanical investment timing plans for the purpose of obtaining objective test results. Although a mechanical application of the liquidity investment timing rules yielded good comparative results, they were not perfect. There was some variation in the leads of monetary changes over stock price changes in the past, and they will undoubtedly persist in the future. In view of the long-term empirical pattern and the plausible explanation presented for this relationship, there is good reason for believing liquidity effects will continue to be important in the future. Judgment, rather than a mechanical plan, must be exercised in applying the principle in future markets. It should be emphasized that liquidity changes are useful in timing only those stock market fluctuations which are associated with business cycles. Although analysis of monetary change and application to investment timing decisions will probably improve overall investment results, this approach does not assure perfection. Perhaps someday such an approach will be devised, but in the meantime, investors must continue to make decisions in the light of imperfect knowledge and understanding. Although there can be no certainty that business and stock price fluctuations will continue in the future, the prudent investor must assume that to be the case. If economic and stock price stability becomes even better in future years, analysis of monetary change is unlikely to improve investment results. However, past patterns suggest no loss will result. Application of monetary principles to investment decisions promises to be a fruitful means of minimizing cyclical risk. It provides prudent insurance against serious error, and will strengthen confidence in investment decisions. If a better comprehension of the effects of monetary change on financial markets results from this book, its basic objective will have been achieved even if extreme volatility in economic and financial markets is avoided in the future.

IX

Effect of Brokerage Charges and Capital Gains Taxes

EFFECT ON INVESTMENT RESULTS

BROKERAGE FEES and capital gains taxes were omitted from consideration in the foregoing investment tests in order to simplify computations. But in the real world, such convenient conventions do not make these investment costs disappear. Inclusion of fees and taxes would have reduced the overall benefits of each of the plans. It is probable, however, that inclusion of income would have more than offset the omitted costs.

Nonetheless, it is clear that inclusion of these costs would have had a differential effect on the plans considered, so that the comparative results would have been affected. For example, the all-stock buy-and-hold program would have fared better relative to each of the other plans considered, since no brokerage costs were incurred in shifting investment funds, and no capital gains taxes would have been paid until liquidation of the fund. Furthermore, since all the delayed adjustment plans appreciated much more than either the all-stock fund or the annual adjustment fund, more brokerage fees and more capital gains taxes would have been incurred. This is tantamount to admitting that the costs of operating successful funds which grow are greater than are the costs of operating less successful investments which appreciate less. The following brokerage fee schedule presents the minimum commission rates on the New York Stock Exchange.

TABLE 19
MINIMUM COMMISSION RATES
NEW YORK STOCK EXCHANGE

Amount of Money Invested	MINIMUM COMMISSION	
	Odd Lots*	Round Lots
Under $100	As mutually agreed	As mutually agreed
$100 to $399	2% + $ 1	2% + $ 3
$400 to $2,399	1% + $ 5	1% + $ 7
$2,400 to $4,999	$\frac{1}{2}$% + $17	$\frac{1}{2}$% + $19
$5,000 and above	$\frac{1}{10}$% + $37	$\frac{1}{10}$% + $39

Source: Merrill Lynch, Pierce, Fenner & Smith.
*Usually 1 to 99 shares.

CAPITAL GAINS TAX EFFECTS ON INVESTMENT DECISIONS

But many investors are convinced that capital gains taxes have a serious detrimental effect on investment decisions and results. A survey of investor opinion by the New York Stock Exchange disclosed the following results:[1]

If the maximum capital gains tax were reduced to 20%, the $29 billion additional unlocked capital would bring about a total of approximately $45 billion released for reinvestment.

The total amount of unlocked capital would rise even more dramatically—up to nearly $78 billion—if the maximum capital gains tax were reduced to 12$\frac{1}{2}$%. Furthermore, Federal tax revenues would more than double—from approximately $1.4 billion to $2.9 billion.

And with the billions of additional dollars that would be released for reinvestment, the prospect may well be for sustained high returns to the Treasury.

---

[1] New York Stock Exchange, "On the Effects of Reducing the Capital Gains Tax Rate," 1961.

Although there can be do doubt that investors consider the
capital gains tax as a major factor affecting investment decisions, there is legitimate doubt as to the correctness of the
widely held view.[2] In the minds of most investors, the existence
of a capital gains tax represents a major deterrent to taking
profits and either switching to another investment medium or
holding liquid funds until better investment buys are available. Since the investment approach developed in this book
involves the taking of gains and reinvestment of funds in
equities at a later and, hopefully, more favorable market
level, the effect of the capital gains tax must be carefully considered. If the detrimental effects of the capital gains tax
are as serious as generally believed, much of the advantage of
proper timing of stock commitments might be dissipated. It
should not be surprising to find that this chapter concludes
otherwise.

The capital gains tax has an effect on each of the two following investment choices: (1) the sale of currently held
securities with the intention of repurchasing the same securities at a lower price, i.e., non-switch decisions; (2) the sale
of currently held securities with the intention of purchasing
alternative investments which are expected to have a superior
price and income performance over a given interval of time,
i.e., switch decisions. Since only the first choice was involved
in the foregoing investment plan tests, discussion will be
limited to that problem. The principles developed for the
choice under consideration are readily adaptable to the second
choice.

Non-switch decisions deal with the possibility of taking advantage of expected short-term fluctuations in the prices of
securities presently held. Such situations arise during the
course of a business cycle, but many investors pass up the

[2] For a detailed discussion of this matter see: Beryl W. Sprinkel and B. Kenneth
West, "Effects of Capital Gains Taxes on Investment Decisions," *Journal of Business*, April, 1962.

opportunity to capitalize on an anticipated temporary market decline not only because of uncertainty that the price decline will actually materialize, but also because capital gains liabilities act as a deterrent to such action.

If a market decline is anticipated, there are two possibilities to be investigated. These depend on expectations as to the market action of the security subsequent to the decline.

1. If the security is expected to remain substantially depressed in price and exhibit poor investment performance relative to other investment alternatives after the decline, clearly, sale of the issue at the current level would maximize profits.

2. The more interesting (and potentially more profitable) possibility to be examined is the situation in which a market decline is expected to be followed by a relatively attractive rise in the price of the security, either surpassing or falling short of the current level. In such circumstances, there seem to be misconceptions among investors as to how the sell or hold alternative should be measured in the face of an expected market decline.

It should be emphasized that for the investor to maximize his profits, judgments as to the future price performance of his holdings must be made on a continuing basis. In the absence of these rather definite expectations, it is not possible to formalize what the impact of capital gains taxes on his decisions should be.

The typical case can best be demonstrated by an example. Suppose an investor held a security with a market value of $100. Suppose, also, that the original cost of this issue was $50, and that the investor's capital gains tax rate was the maximum 25 per cent. Finally, assume that the holder expects the price of this security to fall temporarily to $95, to be followed by an eventual rise to $150, at which point he would sell. Should he hold, or should he sell and buy back at $95? Let us label these alternatives Case A and Case B, respectively.

Case A: Hold to $150 and sell.
                Gross Gain ....$100 ($150-$50)
                Capital Gains Tax 25
                Net Gain ....$ 75

Case B: Sell at $100, pay taxes on gain, buy back at $95, and sell again at
           $150.
    First transaction:
                Sale proceeds $100.00
                Less capital gains tax .... 12.50 ($50 × 0.25)
                Reinvestable funds ....$ 87.50
                Net gain .... 37.50 ($50 − $12.50)

Second transaction: Invest $87.50 at price of $95
$$\text{Percentage gain---}\frac{150 - 95}{95} = 57.9\%$$
                Gross gain—$87.50 × 57.9% $50.66
                Capital gains tax—$50.66 × 0.25 .... 12.67
                Net gain on second transaction $37.99

        Total profits = $37.99 + $37.50 = $75.49

In the example above, the investor would obtain greater net
gains by following the procedure in Case B. *It will be noted
that a market decline of only 40 per cent of the tax liability
and 10 per cent of the total gain yielded these results. This
result will be surprising to those who believe the market value
of a particular holding must decline by at least as much as
the tax liability before sale and repurchase at the lower level
becomes profitable.*[3]

---

[3] Although the algebra is a little tedious, it is possible to generalize this problem and find the break-even point. That is, given the cost, the investor's tax rate,
and his assumptions as to future market performance, it is possible to formalize
the procedure for determining whether to sell and buy back at a lower level or to
hold to the second sell point. This can be accomplished by equating the profits if
held with the profits which would result if a sale were made and the security were
repurchased at the lower level.

    For the purposes of this analysis, let: C = original cost; M = current market;
M_2 = level to which market price is expected to fall in interim; M_3 = expected
market at second sell point; R = reinvestable funds after payment of capital
gains taxes.

    It can be demonstrated that for a sale and repurchase to be profitable, the
ratio of the current market value to reinvestable funds must be smaller than the
ratio of the expected percentage rise from M_2 to M_3 divided by the percentage increase expected from M to M_3, i. e., $M/R < \%$ rise from M_2 to $M_3/\%$ rise from
M to M_3. The following table gives the proper decision under two assumptions
as to the expected interim market decline in the example used previously.

Expected repurchase point	Ratio, Current Market to reinvestable funds	Ratio, % rise from M_2 to M_3/% rise from M to M_3	Indicated Decision
$97.00	1.143	1.093	Hold
94.00	1.143	1.191	Sell & repurchase

The derivable break-even point under the above assumptions is $95.48. From these relationships, several generalizations can be established: (1) The higher M_3, the lower must M_2 be for the investor to break even. (2) the higher the capital gains tax rate, the lower must M_2 be for the investor to break even. (3) the higher the current market, the higher M_2 may be for the investor to break even.

A thorough analysis of the impact of the capital gains tax would involve consideration of several complicating factors: (1) In certain situations, the marginal capital gains tax rate can be in excess of 25 per cent but in most cases is less than 25 per cent. (2) If stocks are sold before holding six months, the gain must be reported as income subject to full income tax rates. (3) If an investor chooses to sell and later repurchase a stock, his income stream will differ from that which would have been experienced if the security were to be held straight through the price dip. (4) Because of the altered timing of the flows introduced by the income stream consideration, precise measurement of the alternatives necessitates a discounting of the income streams (including capital gains) to arrive at an accurate present value of the anticipated income flow alternatives. (5) Brokerage costs also must be taken into account if a sale and repurchase is contemplated. These complications modify but do not alter the basic conclusions.

SUMMARY OF CONCLUSIONS

Capital gains taxes clearly reduce the investor's flexibility in taking advantage of security price fluctuations and in switching to alternative investments. However, investors frequently overestimate the extent of the "lock in" effect. A stock need not decline by a percentage equal to the capital gains tax rate after sale before the investor is even, as is often naively stated. More important, a stock need not decline by the full amount of the existing capital gains tax liability for a sale and repurchase to be profitable. As demonstrated in the example, a sale and repurchase in anticipation of a decline in price of less than one-half of the tax liability may be profitable. It was argued that a sale and repurchase would prove profitable if the ratio of the current market value to reinvestable funds is smaller than the ratio of the percentage rise from the repurchase point (to the ultimate sale point) divided by the percentage increase from the current price (to the ultimate sale point).

The investor frequently forgets that a contingent tax liability exists whether or not a capital gain is actually realized. The tax must eventually be paid unless the security is held until death and the estate benefits from a lower tax rate, or unless the security is given away and the estate benefits from gift taxes. By not realizing a gain, an investor in effect enjoys any income or further capital gain which may accrue to that portion of his assets which represent a contingent capital gains tax. However, a sale and repurchase is profitable so long as the percentage rise from the buy-back price to the final sale price is sufficiently large to offset the reduced capital available for investment after payment of taxes. Although the payment of capital gains taxes will significantly reduce investment results, the existence of the tax will not seriously affect the correctness of a particular investment decision.

All these alternatives can be affected by various complicating factors, including income differentials, brokerage charges, and shifting marginal tax rates. However, these factors can be taken into account. Notwithstanding the existence of these considerations, the basic premise still stands. The impact of capital gains taxes on investment decisions has been overemphasized by many investors. It is also clear that the existence of capital gains taxes will not seriously dissipate the investment advantage of basing investment decisions upon changes in liquidity as measured by changes in the rate of monetary growth.

X

In the End

LET US briefly summarize the evidence and arguments that have consumed the foregoing pages.

1. Changes in the growth rate of the stock of money, i.e., liquidity, exert a pervasive and usually decisive effect on the business cycle and the trend in stock prices, particularly the prices of cyclically sensitive stocks.

2. The impulse of changing monetary growth influences aggregate economic activity and asset prices through the efforts of holders of money to equate their demand for money with the existing stock of money.

3. An understanding of our monetary system with particular emphasis on the relationship between the Federal Reserve and commercial banking systems is crucial in understanding the forces determining changes in the rate of monetary growth.

4. Careful analysis of published data on the banking system and economic activity will permit an able analyst to determine turning points in monetary growth. An attempt to apply this tool mechanically without first understanding basic monetary theory, monetary institutions, and monetary policy will almost certainly lead to disaster.

5. The monetary analyst can best detect and measure the effects of monetary policy action by reviewing policy statements of Federal Reserve officials, and by observing current changes in the stock of money, adjusted total bank reserves, and, to a lesser extent, free reserves.

6. An understanding of the business cycle process, the relation of leading, coincident, and lagging indicators, as well as the strengths and limitations of the indicator approach will provide a useful supplement to the monetary thesis presented in this book.

7. The informed investor can adapt the money-stock price relation to investment policy in such a way as to improve investment results on both a capital appreciation and income basis. In the past, monetary change has failed to portend stock price fluctuations not associated with business cycle fluctuations.

8. Furthermore, if business cycle and associated equity price fluctuations become even less significant in future years, little will be gained from adopting any investment timing device. In other words, if no problem exists, no solution is needed. Therefore, a prudent investor may consider this monetary approach to timing stock investments as an additional insurance against cyclical risks which may or may not develop. If severe cyclical fluctuations are avoided, the monetary approach developed in this book is unlikely to prove costly. If fluctuations prove to be severe in future years, monetary analysis should prove to be a valuable investment tool. In any event, monetary analysis can serve to strengthen confidence in investment decisions which must always be taken in the light of imperfect knowledge.

9. The delay of adjustment of stock-bond ratios until the proper monetary indication is given may be applied by either individual or institutional investors with varying investment objectives.

10. Substantial variation of stock-bond ratios over the market cycle will add significantly to overall investment results. The extent of the variation between the limits of 100–0 per cent must depend on the objectives of the investment account. The greater the emphasis on capital gains and maximum average income, the greater should be the variation at action points. The greater the emphasis on income stability, the less the variation should be.

11. Capital gains taxes and brokerage fees will not seriously dissipate the investment advantages of basing investment timing decisions on changes in liquidity as measured by changes in the rate of monetary growth.

In conclusion, it should be repeated that the investment principles stressed in the foregoing pages should not be considered to be a gimmick that can be applied without thought or understanding. The better informed the investor is on the economy and the financial markets, the better will be the investment timing decision. There can be no guarantee that past patterns will be repeated in the future. Only subsequent experience can reveal the secrets of the future. Also, the problem of selection remains. Cyclically volatile issues are likely to give best results, but the above plans can be applied to all types of stocks to the extent that their prices reflect changes in the underlying business cycle.

Adoption and successful execution of the above principles does not assure an easy road to wealth and plenty. However, it is hoped the liquidity approach represents a significant additional step toward successful investing.

Appendix A

In order to derive a monetary series unaffected by seasonal movements, seasonally adjusted data for demand deposits + currency were used. In order to remove the secular trend from the data, rates of change were computed, that is, the percentage change this month from last month. For example, if the money stock rose from $100 billion last month to $101 billion this month, the rate of change was +1 per cent. If on the other hand it fell from $100 billion to $99 billion, the rate of change was —1 per cent.

Unfortunately month to month changes in the stock of money are erratic, and observation of only the monthly rate of change sometimes makes it difficult to detect the prevailing trend. Consequently a six months' moving average of the monthly rate of change was computed. The six months' moving average reduces the sensitivity of the monetary growth rate series but removes much of the erratic movement. The six months' moving average was computed by averaging the monthly rate of growth for the past six months. The following month, the data for the latest month was added and the seven month old data was removed and a new average six month rate of growth was computed. This procedure was followed for each month. Since, for some purposes, an annual rate of change was desired, each of the six months' average rates of change were converted to average annual rates of change by multiplying by twelve. The annualized six-month moving average rates of change in the stock of money were plotted on charts reflecting the monetary growth rate. The resulting series is seasonally adjusted, reasonably free of erratic movements, yet sensitive to broad cyclical movements. The above procedure was followed in deriving the data for all charts containing the rate of growth in the money stock.

Monetary stock data for the period prior to 1946 were courteously provided by Milton Friedman and Anna Schwartz. A monthly, seasonally adjusted official series does not exist. The data used for the period 1946 to August 1962 was the official series available prior to August 1962 when a modestly revised postwar series was issued. The new series is used subsequent to August 1962. The investment tests conducted in Chapters 7 and 8 used postwar data available prior to the August 1962 revision since that was the data initially available.

The following table presents the stock of money data from 1914 to 1963. Also the monthly rate of change and the annualized six-month moving average rate of change are presented. For the postwar period July 1947 to August 1962 both the old and the new series are listed.

STOCK OF MONEY AND RATES OF GROWTH
(Seas. Adj.--$ Billions)

1914

	Currency + D.D. Adj.	% Monthly Change	6 Mo.* Avg. (An. Rate)
J			
F			
M			
A			
M			
J	11.2		
J	11.2	0	
A	11.3	.89	
S	11.5	1.76	
O	11.4	- .87	
N	11.3	- .87	
D	11.3		1.8

1915

	Currency + D.D. Adj.	% Monthly Change	6 Mo.* Avg. (An. Rate)
J	11.4	.89	3.6
F	11.5	.88	3.6
M	11.6	.88	1.8
A	11.6	0	3.5
M	11.7	.86	7.1
J	11.8	.85	8.8
J	11.9	.84	8.6
A	12.0	.84	8.5
S	12.6	5.00	16.8
O	12.9	2.38	21.5
N	12.9	0	19.8
D	13.1	1.55	21.2

1916

	Currency + D.D. Adj.	% Monthly Change	6 Mo.* Avg. (An. Rate)
J	13.4	2.29	24.1
F	13.6	1.49	25.4
M	13.7	.73	16.9
A	13.8	.72	13.6
M	13.9	.72	15.6
J	14.0	.71	13.3
J	14.2	1.42	11.6
A	14.4	1.40	11.4
S	14.7	2.08	14.0
O	14.9	1.36	15.4
N	15.1	1.34	16.7
D	15.3	1.32	17.9

1917

	Currency + D.D. Adj.	% Monthly Change	6 Mo.* Avg. (An. Rate)
J	15.7	2.61	20.3
F	15.9	1.27	19.9
M	16.1	1.25	18.4
A	16.3	1.24	18.1
M	16.5	1.22	17.9
J	16.6	.60	16.4
J	16.9	1.80	14.8
A	17.1	1.18	14.6
S	17.0	- .59	10.9
O	16.8	-1.18	6.1
N	17.0	1.19	6.0
D	18.0	5.88	16.3

1918

	Currency + D.D. Adj.	% Monthly Change	6 Mo.* Avg. (An. Rate)
J	17.8	-1.12	10.8
F	17.5	-1.69	5.0
M	18.1	3.42	13.0
A	18.2	.55	16.4
M	17.6	-3.30	7.4
J	18.0	2.27	0.2
J	18.2	1.11	4.7
A	18.6	2.19	12.5
S	18.5	- .54	4.3
O	18.9	2.16	7.8
N	19.4	2.64	19.7
D	20.4	5.15	25.4

1919

	Currency + D.D. Adj.	% Monthly Change	6 Mo.* Avg. (An. Rate)
J	20.0	-1.97	19.3
F	19.7	-1.50	11.9
M	20.4	3.55	20.0
A	20.7	1.47	18.7
M	20.7	0	13.3
J	21.0	1.44	6.0
J	21.5	2.38	14.6
A	21.7	.93	19.6
S	22.0	1.38	15.2
O	22.4	1.81	15.8
N	22.6	.89	15.7
D	23.1	2.21	19.2

1920

	Currency + D.D. Adj.	% Monthly Change	6 Mo.* Avg. (An. Rate)
J	22.9	- .87	12.7
F	23.3	1.74	14.3
M	23.6	1.28	13.9
A	23.5	- .43	7.2
M	23.5	0	7.9
J	23.4	- .43	2.6
J	23.4	0	4.3
A	23.3	- .43	0
S	23.2	- .43	- 3.5
O	23.0	- .87	- 4.3
N	22.6	-1.74	- 7.8
D	22.8	.88	- 5.2

1921

	Currency + D.D. Adj.	% Monthly Change	6 Mo.* Avg. (An. Rate)
J	22.2	-2.64	-10.4
F	22.0	- .91	-11.4
M	21.5	-2.28	-15.1
A	21.2	-1.40	-16.2
M	21.2	0	-12.7
J	20.8	-1.89	-18.2
J	20.5	-1.45	-15.8
A	20.5	0	-14.0
S	20.3	- .98	-11.6
O	20.4	.49	- 7.7
N	20.4	0	- 7.7
D	20.3	- .50	- 4.9

Source: Data prior to 1946 supplied by Milton Friedman and Anna Schwartz. Data 1946 to 1948, Federal Reserve Board release G.7, 1948 to present Federal Reserve Board release J.3.

*Six-month moving average of the monthly % changes; multiplied by 12 to get an annual rate. Data is on a daily average.

STOCK OF MONEY AND RATES OF GROWTH
(Seas. Adj.--$ Billions)

1922	Currency + D.D. Adj.	% Monthly Change	6 Mo.* Avg. (An. Rate)
J	20.1	- .99	- 4.0
F	20.4	1.49	- 1.0
M	20.4	0	1.0
A	21.0	2.94	6.8
M	21.2	.95	7.3
J	21.4	.94	13.7
J	21.5	.47	11.8
A	21.5	0	11.8
S	21.8	1.40	8.5
O	21.9	.46	7.6
N	21.8	- .46	4.7
D	22.5	3.21	10.2

1923	Currency + D.D. Adj.	% Monthly Change	6 Mo.* Avg. (An. Rate)
J	22.4	- .45	8.3
F	22.5	.45	9.2
M	22.1	-1.78	2.9
A	22.4	1.36	4.7
M	22.6	.89	7.3
J	22.5	- .44	0.1
J	22.4	- .45	0.1
A	22.3	- .45	- 1.8
S	22.4	.45	2.8
O	22.5	.45	1.0
N	22.5	0	- 0.8
D	22.6	.44	0.8

1924	Currency + D.D. Adj.	% Monthly Change	6 Mo.* Avg. (An. Rate)
J	22.4	- .89	0
F	22.4	0	1.0
M	22.4	0	0
A	22.6	.89	- 2.6
M	22.7	.44	- 1.8
J	23.0	1.32	0
J	23.3	1.30	4.3
A	23.6	1.29	7.0
S	23.8	.85	8.6
O	23.9	.42	11.3
N	24.3	1.67	13.7
D	24.1	- .82	9.5

1925	Currency + D.D. Adj.	% Monthly Change	6 Mo.* Avg. (An. Rate)
J	24.4	1.24	9.4
F	24.6	.82	8.4
M	24.5	- .41	5.9
A	24.7	.82	6.6
M	24.9	.81	4.9
J	25.1	.80	8.2
J	25.2	.40	6.5
A	25.7	1.98	8.8
S	25.9	.78	13.6
O	25.9	0	12.0
N	25.8	- .39	9.5
D	25.7	- .39	7.2

1926	Currency + D.D. Adj.	% Monthly Change	6 Mo.* Avg. (An. Rate)
J	25.7	0	6.4
F	25.9	.78	4.0
M	25.8	- .39	1.7
A	25.6	- .78	0.1
M	25.9	1.17	0.8
J	25.9	0	1.6
J	25.6	-1.16	- 0.8
A	25.7	.39	- 1.6
S	25.6	- .39	- 1.6
O	25.4	- .78	- 1.6
N	25.4	0	- 3.8
D	25.1	-1.18	- 6.2

1927	Currency + D.D. Adj.	% Monthly Change	6 Mo.* Avg. (An. Rate)
J	25.2	.40	- 3.1
F	25.4	.79	- 2.3
M	25.5	.39	- 0.7
A	25.5	0	0.8
M	25.9	1.56	4.0
J	25.6	1.16	8.6
J	25.6	0	7.8
A	25.7	.39	7.1
S	25.5	.78	7.8
O	25.6	.39	8.6
N	26.0	1.56	8.5
D	25.4	-2.31	1.7

1928	Currency + D.D. Adj.	% Monthly Change	6 Mo.* Avg. (An. Rate)
J	25.8	1.57	4.8
F	25.9	.39	4.8
M	25.9	0	3.2
A	26.3	1.54	5.5
M	26.1	.76	3.8
J	25.5	-2.30	3.8
J	25.7	.78	2.3
A	25.5	- .78	0
S	25.7	.78	1.6
O	25.9	.78	0
N	26.1	.77	0
D	26.1	0	4.7

1929	Currency + D.D. Adj.	% Monthly Change	6 Mo.* Avg. (An. Rate)
J	25.8	-1.15	- 0.8
F	25.9	.39	3.1
M	26.0	.39	2.4
A	26.1	.38	1.6
M	25.8	-1.15	- 1.6
J	26.0	.78	- 0.7
J	26.4	1.54	4.7
A	26.2	- .76	2.4
S	26.1	- .38	0.8
O	27.9	6.90	13.9
N	25.2	-9.68	- 3.2
D	26.1	3.57	2.4

STOCK OF MONEY AND RATES OF GROWTH
(Seas. Adj.--$ Billions)

1930

	Currency + D.D. Adj.	% Monthly Change	6 Mo.* Avg. (An. Rate)
J	25.3	-3.07	- 6.8
F	25.6	1.19	- 3.0
M	26.0	1.56	1.0
A	25.6	-1.54	-16.0
M	25.0	-2.34	- 1.3
J	25.0	0	- 8.4
J	25.1	.40	- 1.4
A	24.8	-1.20	- 6.2
S	24.7	-.40	-10.2
O	24.7	0	- 7.1
N	23.8	-3.65	- 9.7
D	24.6	3.36	- 3.0

1931

	Currency + D.D. Adj.	% Monthly Change	6 Mo.* Avg. (An. Rate)
J	24.3	-1.22	- 6.2
F	24.4	.41	- 3.0
M	24.5	.40	- 1.4
A	24.0	-2.05	- 5.5
M	23.6	-1.67	- 1.6
J	23.6	0	- 8.3
J	23.5	-.43	- 6.7
A	23.1	-1.71	-10.9
S	23.1	0	-11.5
O	22.4	-3.04	-13.7
N	22.1	-1.34	-13.1
D	21.6	-2.27	-17.6

1932

	Currency + D.D. Adj.	% Monthly Change	6 Mo.* Avg. (An. Rate)
J	21.2	-1.86	-20.4
F	21.0	- .95	-19.0
M	20.8	- .96	-20.9
A	20.6	- .97	-16.7
M	20.2	-1.95	-17.9
J	20.2	0	-13.4
J	19.9	-1.49	-12.6
A	19.9	0	-10.7
S	19.9	0	- 7.7
O	20.0	.50	- 5.9
N	20.3	1.50	1.1
D	20.1	- .99	- 0.7

1933

	Currency + D.D. Adj.	% Monthly Change	6 Mo.* Avg. (An. Rate)
J	20.3	.99	4.0
F	19.7	-2.96	- 1.9
M	18.8	-2.90	- 7.7
A	18.8	0	- 8.8
M	19.2	2.12	- 7.4
J	18.9	-1.57	- 8.6
J	18.8	- .53	-11.5
A	18.8	0	- 5.5
S	18.9	.53	1.1
O	19.0	.53	1.9
N	19.3	1.57	1.1
D	19.5	1.03	6.2

1934

	Currency + D.D. Adj.	% Monthly Change	6 Mo.* Avg. (An. Rate)
J	19.7	1.02	9.4
F	20.3	3.04	15.5
M	20.8	2.46	19.3
A	20.9	.48	19.2
M	21.0	.47	16.9
J	21.1	.47	15.8
J	21.6	2.36	18.6
A	22.1	2.31	17.2
S	22.0	- .46	11.3
O	22.5	2.27	14.9
N	23.0	2.22	18.4
D	22.7	-1.31	14.8

1935

	Currency + D.D. Adj.	% Monthly Change	6 Mo.* Avg. (An. Rate)
J	23.6	3.96	17.9
F	24.4	3.38	20.2
M	24.3	- .41	20.3
A	24.6	1.23	18.1
M	24.8	.81	15.4
J	25.2	1.61	21.1
J	25.4	.79	14.9
A	26.8	5.51	19.1
S	26.4	-1.50	16.9
O	26.7	1.13	16.7
N	27.3	2.24	19.6
D	27.0	-1.10	14.2

1936

	Currency + D.D. Adj.	% Monthly Change	6 Mo.* Avg. (An. Rate)
J	27.1	.37	13.3
F	27.6	1.84	5.9
M	27.6	0	9.0
A	28.2	2.17	11.0
M	29.0	2.83	12.2
J	29.7	2.41	19.2
J	29.8	.33	19.1
A	29.7	- .34	14.4
S	30.2	1.68	18.1
O	30.1	- .34	13.2
N	30.4	.99	9.5
D	30.8	1.31	7.3

1937

	Currency + D.D. Adj.	% Monthly Change	6 Mo.* Avg. (An. Rate)
J	30.6	- .65	- 5.3
F	30.9	.98	- 7.9
M	31.1	.64	- 5.9
A	31.0	- .33	- 5.9
M	30.6	-1.30	- 1.3
J	30.6	0	- 1.3
J	30.5	.33	0.6
A	30.3	- .66	- 2.6
S	30.1	- .67	- 5.3
O	29.5	-2.00	- 8.5
N	29.3	- .68	- 7.3
D	29.0	-1.03	- 9.5

STOCK OF MONEY AND RATES OF GROWTH
(Seas. Adj.--$ Billions)

	Currency + D.D. Adj.	% Monthly Change	6 Mo.* Avg. (An. Rate)		Currency + D.D. Adj.	% Monthly Change	6 Mo.* Avg. (An. Rate)		Currency + D.D. Adj.	% Monthly Change	6 Mo.* Avg. (An. Rate)		Currency + D.D. Adj.	% Monthly Change	6 Mo.* Avg. (An. Rate)
1938				**1940**				**1942**				**1944**			
J	29.3	1.03	- 8.0	J	36.5	1.38	17.3	J	49.4	2.70	11.8	J	78.3	-1.76	8.3
F	29.5	.68	- 5.4	F	37.0	1.36	15.2	F	50.1	1.41	14.1	F	79.3	1.27	1.3
M	29.6	.33	- 3.4	M	37.6	1.62	13.9	M	50.7	1.19	14.3	M	80.7	1.76	23.5
A	29.4	-.68	- 0.7	A	37.4	-.54	11.0	A	52.0	2.56	19.9	A	82.4	2.10	24.4
M	29.1	-1.03	- 1.4	M	38.2	2.13	7.3	M	53.0	1.92	20.8	M	84.5	2.54	20.0
J	29.2	-.34	1.3	J	38.8	1.57	15.0	J	53.4	.75	21.1	J	83.4	-1.31	9.2
J	29.5	1.02	1.3	J	39.2	1.03	14.3	J	55.3	3.55	22.7	J	84.1	.83	14.4
A	30.2	2.37	4.7	A	39.4	.51	12.6	A	56.6	2.35	24.6	A	86.7	3.09	18.0
S	30.6	1.32	6.7	S	39.9	1.26	11.9	S	58.0	2.47	27.2	S	88.4	1.96	18.5
O	30.9	.98	10.0	O	40.5	1.50	16.0	O	60.0	3.44	28.9	O	90.9	2.82	15.8
N	31.5	1.94	16.0	N	41.1	1.48	14.8	N	61.1	1.83	28.8	N	93.2	2.53	15.8
D	31.7	.63	16.6	D	41.9	1.94	15.5	D	62.5	2.29	31.9	D	90.6	-2.79	19.3
1939				**1941**				**1943**				**1945**			
J	31.6	- .32	13.8	J	42.6	1.67	16.7	J	64.3	2.88	30.5	J	93.7	3.42	22.1
F	31.6	0	9.0	F	43.8	2.81	21.4	F	67.1	4.35	34.6	F	95.3	1.70	19.3
M	32.0	1.26	9.0	M	44.5	1.59	22.0	M	69.1	2.98	35.5	M	97.3	2.09	19.6
A	32.3	.93	8.9	A	44.7	.44	19.9	A	68.3	-1.16	28.3	A	98.1	.82	15.6
M	32.5	.61	6.2	M	45.6	2.01	20.9	M	69.1	1.17	25.1	M	98.7	.61	11.8
J	32.6	.30	5.5	J	45.4	-.44	16.2	J	72.9	5.49	31.4	J	97.6	-1.12	15.0
J	33.5	2.76	11.8	J	46.6	2.64	18.1	J	75.7	3.84	33.4	J	99.1	1.53	11.3
A	34.3	2.38	16.4	A	46.7	.21	13.0	A	79.3	4.75	34.2	A	100.3	1.21	10.3
S	35.1	2.33	18.6	S	47.2	1.07	11.9	S	71.9	-9.34	9.5	S	101.7	1.39	8.9
O	35.4	.85	18.5	O	47.1	- .22	10.6	O	73.1	1.66	15.1	O	102.4	.68	8.5
N	36.4	2.82	22.9	N	47.8	1.48	9.5	N	76.4	4.51	21.8	N	103.0	.58	8.5
D	36.0	-1.10	20.0	D	48.1	.62	11.6	D	79.7	4.31	19.4	D	102.2	- .78	9.2

STOCK OF MONEY AND RATES OF GROWTH
(Seas. Adj.--$ Billions)

	Currency + D.D. Adj.	% Monthly Change	6 Mo.* Avg. (An. Rate)
1946			
J	101.9	- .30	5.6
F	103.1	1.17	5.5
M	102.8	- .30	2.1
A	105.0	2.14	3.0
M	106.1	1.04	5.9
J	106.8	.65	8.8
J	107.3	.46	10.3
A	107.3	0	8.0
S	107.7	.37	9.3
O	107.9	.18	5.4
N	107.9	0	3.3
D	107.6	- .28	1.5
1947			
J	107.5	- .10	0.3
F	107.5	0	0.3
M	108.3	.74	1.1
A	108.8	.46	1.6
M	108.9	.09	1.8
J	109.3	.36	3.1
1947 Data Revised — Oct. 1960, p. 115, FRB			
J	108.7		
F	108.9	.18	
M	109.6	.64	
A	110.3	.64	
M	110.8	.45	
J	111.4	.54	
J	111.5	.09	5.1
A	111.7	.18	5.1
S	111.9	.18	4.2
O	112.0	.09	3.1
N	112.3	.27	1.7
D	112.2	- .09	1.4

	Currency + D.D. Adj.	% Monthly Change	6 Mo.* Avg. (An. Rate)
1948			
J	112.6	.36	2.0
F	112.3	- .27	1.1
M	111.9	- .36	0
A	111.5	- .36	0.9
M	111.2	- .27	- 2.0
J	111.3	.09	- 1.6
J	111.4	.09	- 2.2
A	111.5	.09	- 1.4
S	111.3	- .18	- 1.1
O	111.2	- .09	- 0.5
N	110.9	- .27	- 0.5
D	110.7	- .18	- 1.1
1949			
J	110.2	- .45	- 2.2
F	110.2	0	- 2.3
M	110.2	0	- 2.0
A	110.3	.09	- 1.6
M	110.5	.18	- 0.7
J	110.4	- .09	- 0.5
J	110.3	- .09	- 0.2
A	110.1	- .09	- 0.2
S	110.0	- .18	- 0.4
O	109.9	- .09	- 0.7
N	109.8	- .09	- 1.3
D	110.1	.27	- 0.5
1950			
J	110.3	.18	0
F	110.8	.45	1.3
M	111.3	.45	2.3
A	112.1	.72	4.0
M	112.5	.35	4.8
J	112.8	.27	4.8
J	113.4	.53	5.5
A	113.9	.44	5.5
S	114.1	.18	5.0
O	114.6	.44	4.4
N	114.8	.18	4.1
D	115.3	.44	4.4
1951			
J	115.8	.43	4.2
F	116.1	.26	4.0
M	116.7	.52	4.5
A	116.8	.09	3.8
M	117.1	.26	4.0
J	117.6	.43	4.0
J	117.9	.26	3.6
A	118.7	.68	4.5
S	119.4	.59	4.6
O	120.2	.67	5.8
N	121.3	.92	7.1
D	121.9	.49	7.2

	Currency + D.D. Adj.	% Monthly Change	6 Mo.* Avg. (An. Rate)
1952			
J	122.5	.49	7.8
F	123.0	.41	7.1
M	123.1	.08	6.1
A	123.4	.24	5.3
M	123.7	.24	3.9
J	124.3	.49	3.9
J	124.4	.08	3.1
A	124.8	.32	2.9
S	125.4	.48	3.7
O	125.8	.32	3.9
N	126.2	.32	4.0
D	126.4	.16	3.4
1953			
J	126.5	.08	3.4
F	126.7	.16	3.0
M	127.3	.47	3.0
A	127.6	.24	2.9
M	127.7	.08	2.4
J	127.8	.08	2.2
J	127.9	.08	2.2
A	128.0	.08	2.1
S	127.9	- .08	1.0
O	128.0	.08	0.6
N	128.0	0	0.5
D	128.1	.08	0.5

STOCK OF MONEY AND RATES OF GROWTH
(Seas. Adj.--$ Billions)

1954

Month	Currency + D.D. Adj.	% Monthly Change	6 Mo.* Avg. (An. Rate)
J	128.3	.16	0.6
F	128.4	.08	0.6
M	128.5	.08	1.0
A	128.2	-.23	0.3
M	129.0	.62	1.6
J	129.1	.08	1.6
J	129.5	.31	1.9
A	129.9	.31	2.3
S	130.2	.23	2.6
O	130.7	.38	3.9
N	131.4	.54	3.7
D	131.7	.23	4.0

1955

Month	Currency + D.D. Adj.	% Monthly Change	6 Mo.* Avg. (An. Rate)
J	132.3	.46	4.3
F	133.2	.68	5.0
M	133.0	-.15	4.3
A	133.5	.38	4.3
M	133.9	.30	3.8
J	133.9	0	3.3
J	134.2	.22	2.9
A	134.3	.08	1.7
S	134.6	.22	2.4
O	134.6	0	1.6
N	134.3	-.22	0.6
D	134.6	.22	1.0

1956

Month	Currency + D.D. Adj.	% Monthly Change	6 Mo.* Avg. (An. Rate)
J	135.1	.37	1.3
F	135.0	-.08	1.0
M	135.4	.30	1.2
A	135.6	.15	1.5
M	135.4	-.15	1.6
J	135.6	.15	1.5
J	135.4	-.15	0.4
A	135.2	-.15	0.3
S	135.7	.37	0.4
O	135.7	0	0.1
N	136.0	.22	0.9
D	136.5	.37	1.3

1957

Month	Currency + D.D. Adj.	% Monthly Change	6 Mo.* Avg. (An. Rate)
J	136.4	-.08	1.5
F	136.4	0	1.8
M	136.5	.08	1.2
A	136.4	-.08	1.0
M	136.5	.08	0.7
J	136.3	-.15	- 0.3
J	136.4	.08	0
A	136.6	.15	0.3
S	136.2	-.29	- 0.4
O	136.0	-.15	- 0.6
N	135.7	-.22	- 1.2
D	135.5	-.15	- 1.2

1958

Month	Currency + D.D. Adj.	% Monthly Change	6 Mo.* Avg. (An. Rate)
J	135.3	-.15	- 1.6
F	135.8	.22	- 1.5
M	136.5	.52	0.1
A	136.5	0	0.4
M	137.0	.37	1.6
J	138.0	.73	3.4
J	137.7	.22	3.2
A	138.6	.65	4.1
S	139.1	.36	3.7
O	139.6	.36	4.5
N	140.4	.57	4.9
D	140.8	.28	4.0

1959

Month	Currency + D.D. Adj.	% Monthly Change	6 Mo.* Avg. (An. Rate)
J	141.1	.21	4.8
F	141.6	.35	4.3
M	142.0	.28	4.1
A	142.1	.07	3.5
M	142.6	.35	3.1
J	142.7	.07	2.7
J	143.3	.42	3.1
A	142.8	.35	1.7
S	142.8	0	1.1
O	142.4	-.28	0.4
N	142.1	-.21	- 0.7
D	141.5	-.42	- 1.7

1960

Month	Currency + D.D. Adj.	% Monthly Change	6 Mo.* Avg. (An. Rate)
J	141.3	-.14	- 2.8
F	141.1	-.14	- 2.4
M	140.6	-.36	- 3.1
A	140.5	.07	- 2.7
M	139.9	-.43	- 3.1
J	139.5	-.29	- 2.9
J	139.6	.07	- 2.4
A	139.7	.07	- 2.0
S	140.4	.50	0.3
O	140.6	-.14	0.1
N	140.2	-.29	0.4
D	140.4	.14	1.3

1961

Month	Currency + D.D. Adj.	% Monthly Change	6 Mo.* Avg. (An. Rate)
J	140.6	.14	1.4
F	141.2	.42	2.1
M	141.5	.21	1.5
A	142.0	.35	1.9
M	142.1	0	2.5
J	142.0	.07	2.4
J	142.0	.07	2.2
A	141.8	-.14	0.8
S	143.0	.85	2.1
O	143.7	.49	2.4
N	144.1	.28	3.0
D	144.9	.55	3.9

STOCK OF MONEY AND RATES OF GROWTH
(Seas. Adj.--$ Billions)

1962	Currency + D.D. Adj.	% Monthly Change	6 Mo.* Avg. (An. Rate)
J	144.6	- .21	3.6
F	144.4	- .14	3.6
M	144.7	.21	2.4
A	145.7	.69	2.8
M	145.4	- .21	1.8
J	145.3	- .07	0.5
J	145.0	- .21	0.5

Data Revised
Aug. 1962, p. 946, FRB

1947	Currency + D.D. Adj.	% Monthly Change	6 Mo.* Avg. (An. Rate)
J	109.5		
F	109.7	.18	
M	110.4	.64	
A	111.2	.72	
M	111.7	.44	
J	112.1	.35	
J	112.3	.17	5.0
A	112.6	.27	5.2
S	113.0	.36	4.6
O	113.0	0	3.2
N	113.3	.27	2.8
D	113.1	- .18	1.8

1948	Currency + D.D. Adj.	% Monthly Change	6 Mo.* Avg. (An. Rate)
J	113.4	.27	2.0
F	113.2	- .18	1.1
M	112.7	- .44	- 0.5
A	112.3	- .36	- 1.2
M	112.1	- .18	- 2.1
J	112.0	- .09	- 2.0
J	112.2	.18	- 2.1
A	112.3	.09	- 1.6
S	112.2	- .09	- 0.9
O	112.2	0	- 0.2
N	111.8	- .36	- 0.5
D	111.6	- .18	- 0.7

1949	Currency + D.D. Adj.	% Monthly Change	6 Mo.* Avg. (An. Rate)
J	111.2	- .36	- 1.8
F	111.2	0	- 2.0
M	111.3	.09	- 1.6
A	111.4	.09	- 1.4
M	111.5	.09	- 0.5
J	111.3	- .18	- 0.5
J	111.2	- .09	0
A	111.1	- .09	- 0.2
S	110.9	- .18	- 0.7
O	110.9	0	- 0.9
N	110.0	.09	- 0.9
D	111.2	.18	- 0.2

1950	Currency + D.D. Adj.	% Monthly Change	6 Mo.* Avg. (An. Rate)
J	111.5	.27	0.5
F	112.1	.54	1.8
M	112.6	.45	3.1
A	113.3	.62	4.3
M	113.8	.44	5.0
J	114.1	.26	5.2
J	114.7	.53	5.7
A	115.0	.26	5.1
S	115.3	.26	4.7
O	115.7	.35	4.2
N	115.9	.17	3.7
D	116.2	.26	3.7

1951	Currency + D.D. Adj.	% Monthly Change	6 Mo.* Avg. (An. Rate)
J	116.7	.43	3.5
F	117.2	.43	3.8
M	117.6	.34	4.0
A	117.8	.17	3.6
M	118.2	.34	3.9
J	118.6	.34	4.1
J	119.1	.42	4.1
A	119.6	.42	4.1
S	120.4	.67	4.7
O	121.0	.50	5.4
N	122.0	.83	6.4
D	122.7	.57	6.8

1952	Currency + D.D. Adj.	% Monthly Change	6 Mo.* Avg. (An. Rate)
J	123.2	.41	6.8
F	123.6	.32	6.6
M	123.8	.16	5.6
A	124.1	.24	5.1
M	124.5	.32	4.0
J	125.1	.48	3.9
J	125.4	.24	3.5
A	125.7	.24	3.4
S	126.4	.56	4.2
O	126.7	.24	4.2
N	127.1	.32	4.2
D	127.5	.31	3.8

1953	Currency + D.D. Adj.	% Monthly Change	6 Mo.* Avg. (An. Rate)
J	127.3	- .16	3.0
F	127.4	.08	2.7
M	128.0	.47	2.5
A	128.4	.31	2.7
M	128.5	.08	2.2
J	128.5	0	1.6
J	128.6	.08	2.0
A	128.7	.08	2.0
S	128.6	- .08	0.9
O	128.7	.08	0.5
N	128.7	0	0.3
D	128.9	.16	0.6

STOCK OF MONEY AND RATES OF GROWTH
(Seas. Adj.--$ Billions)

1954

	Currency + D.D. Adj.	% Monthly Change	6 Mo.* Avg. (An. Rate)
J	129.0	.08	0.6
F	129.2	.16	0.8
M	129.2	0	1.0
A	128.6	- .47	- 0.1
M	129.8	.93	1.7
J	129.9	.08	1.6
J	130.3	.31	2.0
A	130.7	.31	2.3
S	130.9	.15	2.6
O	131.5	.46	4.5
N	132.1	.46	3.5
D	132.4	.23	3.8

1955

	Currency + D.D. Adj.	% Monthly Change	6 Mo.* Avg. (An. Rate)
J	133.0	.45	4.1
F	133.8	.60	4.7
M	133.7	- .08	4.2
A	134.1	.30	3.9
M	134.4	.23	3.5
J	134.4	0	3.0
J	134.8	.30	2.7
A	134.9	.08	1.7
S	135.1	.15	2.1
O	135.2	.07	1.7
N	134.9	- .22	0.8
D	135.3	.30	1.4

1956

	Currency + D.D. Adj.	% Monthly Change	6 Mo.* Avg. (An. Rate)
J	135.6	.22	1.2
F	135.5	- .07	0.9
M	135.9	.30	1.2
A	136.2	.22	1.5
M	135.8	- .29	1.4
J	136.1	.22	1.2
J	135.9	- .15	0.5
A	135.8	- .07	0.5
S	136.1	.22	0.3
O	136.2	.07	0
N	136.6	.29	1.2
D	136.9	.22	1.2

1957

	Currency + D.D. Adj.	% Monthly Change	6 Mo.* Avg. (An. Rate)
J	136.9	0	1.5
F	137.0	.07	1.7
M	137.1	.07	1.4
A	136.9	- .15	1.0
M	137.0	.07	0.6
J	136.9	- .07	0
J	137.1	.15	0.2
A	137.0	- .07	0
S	136.7	- .22	- 0.6
O	136.4	- .22	- 0.7
N	136.2	- .15	- 1.2
D	135.9	- .22	- 1.5

1958

	Currency + D.D. Adj.	% Monthly Change	6 Mo.* Avg. (An. Rate)
J	135.6	- .22	- 2.2
F	136.3	.52	- 1.0
M	136.5	.15	0.3
A	137.0	.37	0.9
M	137.6	.44	2.1
J	138.5	.65	3.8
J	138.4	- .07	4.1
A	139.1	.51	4.1
S	139.5	.29	4.4
O	140.1	.43	4.5
N	140.8	.50	4.6
D	141.2	.28	3.9

1959

	Currency + D.D. Adj.	% Monthly Change	6 Mo.* Avg. (An. Rate)
J	141.6	.28	4.5
F	142.0	.28	4.1
M	142.6	.42	4.4
A	142.7	.07	3.7
M	143.2	.35	3.4
J	143.4	.14	3.1
J	144.0	.42	3.4
A	143.5	- .35	2.1
S	143.2	- .21	0.8
O	142.9	- .21	0.3
N	142.7	- .14	- 0.7
D	142.1	- .42	- 1.8

1960

	Currency + D.D. Adj.	% Monthly Change	6 Mo.* Avg. (An. Rate)
J	141.8	- .21	- 3.1
F	141.4	- .28	- 2.9
M	141.1	- .21	- 2.9
A	140.9	- .14	- 2.8
M	140.4	- .35	- 3.2
J	140.1	- .21	- 2.8
J	140.4	.21	- 2.0
A	140.9	.36	- 0.7
S	141.0	.07	- 0.1
O	141.1	.07	0.3
N	140.8	- .21	0.6
D	141.2	.28	1.6

1961

	Currency + D.D. Adj.	% Monthly Change	6 Mo.* Avg. (An. Rate)
J	141.5	.21	1.6
F	141.8	.21	1.3
M	142.2	.28	1.7
A	142.5	.21	2.0
M	142.9	.28	2.9
J	142.8	- .07	2.2
J	143.0	.14	2.1
A	142.9	- .07	1.5
S	143.5	.42	1.8
O	144.2	.49	2.4
N	144.9	.49	2.8
D	145.7	.55	4.0

1962

	Currency + D.D. Adj.	% Monthly Change	6 Mo.* Avg. (An. Rate)
J	145.9	.14	4.0
F	145.5	- .28	3.6
M	145.7	.14	3.1
A	146.1	.27	2.6
M	145.7	- .27	1.1
J	145.6	- .07	0.1
J	145.7	.07	- 0.2
A	145.1	- .42	0.6
S	145.3	.14	- 0.6
O	146.1	.55	0
N	146.9	.55	1.6
D	147.9	.68	3.1

1963

	Currency + D.D. Adj.	% Monthly Change	6 Mo.* Avg. (An. Rate)
J	148.7	.54	4.1
F	148.6	- .07	4.8
M	148.9	.20	4.9
A	149.4	.34	4.5
M	149.4	0	3.4
J	149.8	.27	2.6
J	150.7	.60	2.7
A	150.5	- .13	2.6
S	150.9	.27	2.7
O	152.1	.80	3.6
N	153.4	.85	5.3
D	153.5	.07	4.9

Appendix B

THIS APPENDIX includes data for analytical charts the reader may want to duplicate. Data are ommitted for charts regularly published by the Department of Commerce in Business Cycle Conditions and also for Charts 13 through 18 which present summary information on the various investment tests. Since data on the stock of money and its rate of growth are presented in Appendix A, they are ommitted in the compilations which follow. Data for Charts appearing in the text are presented for Charts 1, 2, 3, 7, 10, 11, and 12.

CHARTS 1 AND 12

LIQUIDITY FAVORABLE FOR STOCKS				BUSINESS CYCLES			
SELL DATE		BUY DATE		PEAK		TROUGH	
MAY	1917	AUG.	1918	JAN.	1920	JUL.	1921
MAR.	1920	AUG.	1921	MAY	1923	JUL.	1924
SEP.	1923	JUN.	1924	OCT.	1926	NOV.	1927
FEB.	1926	FEB.	1927	JUN.	1929	MAR.	1933
JAN.	1929	MAY	1932	MAY	1937	JUN.	1938
SEP.	1936	FEB.	1938	NOV.	1948	OCT.	1949
APR.	1946	APR.	1949	JUL.	1953	AUG.	1954
APR.	1953	JAN.	1954	JUL.	1957	APR.	1958
MAY	1956	MAR.	1958	MAY	1960	FEB.	1961
FEB.	1960	JUL.	1960				

CHART 1

PEAKS AND TROUGHS OF MONEY GROWTH

Peaks		% Change	Troughs		% Change
Dec.	1918	25.4	June	1918	0.2
June	1922	13.7	June	1921	-18.2
Nov.	1924	13.7	April	1924	- 2.6
Oct.	1927	8.6	Dec.	1926	- 6.2
June	1935	21.1	Mar.	1932	-20.9
Jan.	1945	22.1	Dec.	1937	- 9.5
Jan.	1952	7.8	Feb.	1949	- 2.3
Feb.	1955	5.0	Nov.	1953	0.5
Nov.	1958	4.9	Jan.	1958	- 1.6
			May	1960	- 3.1

189

CHARTS 1 AND 12

STOCK PRICES

	S & P Industrial		S & P Industrial		S & P Industrial		S & P Industrial
1918		**1922**		**1926**		**1930**	
J	5.25	J	5.46	J	10.04	J	17.13
F	5.46	F	5.57	F	10.10	F	18.06
M	5.31	M	5.78	M	9.38	M	18.73
A	5.32	A	6.20	A	9.06	A	19.93
M	5.53	M	6.52	M	9.12	M	18.60
J	5.54	J	6.46	J	9.59	J	16.68
J	5.62	J	6.43	J	10.06	J	16.41
A	5.66	A	6.59	A	10.52	A	16.33
S	5.57	S	6.82	S	10.67	S	16.21
O	5.79	O	7.03	O	10.46	O	13.84
N	5.91	N	6.67	N	10.58	N	12.97
D	5.84	D	6.72	D	10.84	D	12.17
1919		**1923**		**1927**		**1931**	
J	5.93	J	6.87	J	10.74	J	12.34
F	5.95	F	7.22	F	10.96	F	13.27
M	6.21	M	7.40	M	11.16	M	13.45
A	6.57	A	7.08	A	11.42	A	12.18
M	7.10	M	6.64	M	11.85	M	10.97
J	7.44	J	6.25	J	12.01	J	10.56
J	7.85	J	6.02	J	12.38	J	10.95
A	7.36	A	6.07	A	13.18	A	10.72
S	7.55	S	6.11	S	14.08	S	9.15
O	8.10	O	5.99	O	13.80	O	7.91
N	7.86	N	6.24	N	14.20	N	8.09
D	7.67	D	6.60	D	14.61	D	6.54
1920		**1924**		**1928**		**1932**	
J	7.56	J	6.84	J	14.68	J	6.39
F	6.75	F	6.87	F	14.43	F	6.33
M	7.31	M	6.67	M	15.34	M	6.35
A	7.33	A	6.42	A	16.35	A	4.83
M	6.78	M	6.35	M	16.74	M	4.27
J	6.64	J	6.45	J	15.96	J	3.80
J	6.56	J	6.77	J	16.18	J	4.00
A	6.06	A	7.05	A	16.80	A	5.94
S	6.23	S	6.73	S	18.11	S	6.39
O	6.05	O	6.95	O	18.70	O	5.49
N	5.65	N	7.22	N	19.94	N	5.45
D	5.08	D	7.66	D	19.75	D	5.18
1921		**1925**		**1929**		**1933**	
J	5.35	J	8.13	J	21.22	J	5.35
F	5.31	F	8.25	F	21.12	F	4.74
M	5.17	M	7.95	M	21.68	M	4.93
A	5.23	A	7.91	A	21.62	A	5.75
M	5.40	M	8.16	M	21.70	M	7.41
J	4.83	J	8.36	J	21.55	J	8.61
J	4.72	J	8.66	J	22.95	J	9.40
A	4.57	A	8.75	A	23.89	A	9.15
S	4.72	S	9.02	S	24.68	S	9.37
O	4.86	O	9.41	O	22.26	O	8.49
N	5.23	N	9.79	N	16.44	N	8.92
D	5.50	D	9.87	D	17.03	D	9.16

Source: FRB and Standard & Poor's.

STOCK PRICES

	S & P Industrial		S & P Industrial		S & P Industrial		S & P Industrial
1934		1938		1942		1946	
J	9.56	J	11.10	J	8.95	J	17.34
F	10.11	F	10.89	F	8.67	F	17.38
M	9.63	M	10.22	M	8.24	M	16.85
A	9.86	A	9.81	A	7.93	A	18.02
M	8.88	M	9.78	M	8.01	M	18.04
J	8.96	J	10.07	J	8.47	J	17.85
J	8.60	J	12.12	J	8.82	J	17.42
A	8.41	A	12.29	A	8.76	A	17.12
S	8.22	S	11.81	S	8.84	S	14.65
O	8.31	O	12.98	O	9.45	O	14.35
N	8.70	N	12.96	N	9.56	N	14.20
D	8.81	D	12.63	D	9.68	D	14.58
1935		1939		1943		1947	
J	8.88	J	12.30	J	10.22	J	14.69
F	8.72	F	12.12	F	10.81	F	15.31
M	8.19	M	12.09	M	11.13	M	14.73
A	8.67	A	10.56	A	11.44	A	14.23
M	9.40	M	10.91	M	11.87	M	14.02
J	9.64	J	11.11	J	12.14	J	14.58
J	10.14	J	11.37	J	12.29	Revised 10-1-62	
A	10.71	A	11.15	A	11.66	J	15.48
S	11.01	S	12.56	S	11.91	A	15.15
O	11.39	O	12.60	O	11.78	S	14.76
N	12.43	N	12.35	N	11.25	O	15.19
D	12.38	D	12.06	D	11.42	N	15.15
						D	14.93
1936		1940		1944		1948	
J	12.96	J	11.95	J	11.78	J	14.60
F	13.71	F	11.87	F	11.63	F	13.88
M	14.12	M	11.84	M	11.95	M	14.07
A	14.20	A	11.94	A	11.75	A	15.19
M	13.44	M	10.28	M	11.98	M	15.92
J	13.93	J	9.34	J	12.58	J	16.65
J	14.66	J	9.55	J	12.90	J	16.21
A	14.96	A	9.79	A	12.67	A	15.74
S	15.17	S	10.26	S	12.47	S	15.53
O	16.04	O	10.39	O	12.76	O	16.02
N	16.69	N	10.73	N	12.67	N	15.16
D	16.41	D	10.34	D	12.90	D	15.11
1937		1941		1945		1949	
J	16.87	J	10.30	J	13.23	J	15.23
F	17.51	F	9.64	F	13.63	F	14.57
M	17.52	M	9.73	M	13.63	M	14.72
A	16.45	A	9.43	A	13.94	A	14.66
M	15.74	M	9.27	M	14.44	M	14.51
J	15.26	J	9.66	J	14.58	J	13.69
J	16.18	J	10.19	J	14.23	J	14.55
A	16.45	A	10.14	A	14.39	A	15.04
S	14.12	S	10.21	S	15.43	S	15.20
O	12 04	O	9.81	O	16.03	O	15.62
N	10.82	N	9.41	N	16.41	N	15.86
D	10.68	D	8.86	D	16.73	D	16.29

STOCK PRICES

	S & P Industrial		S & P Industrial		S & P Industrial		S & P Industrial
1950		**1954**		**1958**		**1962**	
J	16.56	J	25.55	J	43.98	J	72.99
F	16.90	F	26.12	F	44.01	F	74.22
M	17.03	M	26.72	M	44.97	M	74.22
A	17.58	A	27.97	A	45.09	A	71.64
M	18.27	M	29.21	M	46.51	M	66.32
J	18.68	J	29.43	J	47.62	J	58.32
J	17.31	J	30.64	J	48.96	J	59.61
A	18.47	A	31.26	A	51.00	A	61.29
S	19.18	S	32.20	S	52.40	S	60.67
O	20.06	O	33.17	O	54.55	O	58.66
N	20.05	N	34.54	N	56.11	N	62.90
D	19.92	D	36.14	D	57.09	D	65.59
1951		**1955**		**1959**		**1963**	
J	21.38	J	36.79	J	59.30	J	68.00
F	22.22	F	38.06	F	58.33	F	68.91
M	21.84	M	37.65	M	59.79	M	68.71
A	22.24	A	39.04	A	62.21	A	72.17
M	22.29	M	38.88	M	62.09	M	73.60
J	21.88	J	41.45	J	61.75	J	73.61
J	22.31	J	44.94	J	64.23	J	72.45
A	23.35	A	44.56	A	63.74	A	74.43
S	23.98	S	46.88	S	61.21	S	76.63
O	23.80	O	44.52	O	61.04	O	77.09
N	23.09	N	47.78	N	61.46	N	76.69
D	23.83	D	48.25	D	63.56	D	78.38
1952		**1956**		**1960**			
J	24.61	J	46.88	J	62.27		
F	24.45	F	47.13	F	59.60		
M	24.04	M	50.59	M	58.71		
A	23.96	A	51.38	A	59.46		
M	23.94	M	49.64	M	58.84		
J	24.66	J	49.38	J	61.06		
J	25.49	J	52.27	J	59.25		
A	25.53	A	51.89	A	59.96		
S	25.06	S	50.15	S	57.96		
O	24.48	O	49.52	O	56.90		
N	25.24	N	48.92	N	58.89		
D	26.29	D	49.79	D	60.22		
1953		**1957**		**1961**			
J	26.45	J	48.43	J	63.20		
F	26.07	F	46.10	F	65.91		
M	26.18	M	46.86	M	67.83		
A	24.84	A	48.06	A	69.64		
M	25.01	M	50.10	M	70.34		
J	24.12	J	51.30	J	69.48		
J	24.41	J	52.54	J	69.15		
A	24.44	A	49.51	A	71.69		
S	23.26	S	47.52	S	70.89		
O	23.96	O	44.43	O	71.42		
N	24.51	N	43.41	N	74.72		
D	24.85	D	43.29	D	75.82		

CHART 2

MEMBER BANK RESERVES
(Millions of Dollars--Seas. Adj.)

	Total* Reserves	Required* Reserves	Reserves Avail. for Pvt. D.D.
1957			
J	16,688	16,174	14,980
F	16,718	16,198	14,992
M	16,692	16,153	14,950
A	16,703	16,178	14,947
M	16,634	16,148	14,867
J	16,663	16,148	14,885
J	16,670	16,136	14,881
A	16,673	16,153	14,872
S	16,646	16,139	14,832
O	16,576	16,093	14,745
N	16,619	16,092	14,772
D	16,586	16,071	14,722
1958			
J	16,627	16,063	14,743
F	16,793	16,222	14,863
M	16,895	16,256	14,926
A	17,078	16,435	15,074
M	17,215	16,526	15,182
J	17,365	16,718	15,306
J	17,372	16,716	15,283
A	17,424	16,822	15,318
S	17,387	16,814	15,274
O	17,358	16,821	15,240
N	17,415	16,893	15,288
D	17,395	16,941	15,258

	Total* Reserves	Required* Reserves	Reserves Avail. for Pvt. D.D.
1959			
J	17,423	16,951	15,269
F	17,420	16,975	15,261
M	17,525	17,059	15,364
A	17,559	17,121	15,392
M	17,617	17,147	15,444
J	17,551	17,105	15,376
J	17,598	17,199	15,423
A	17,530	17,073	15,358
S	17,439	17,010	15,268
O	17,417	16,954	15,246
N	17,390	16,947	15,220
D	17,277	16,858	15,109
1960			
J	17,290	16,772	15,128
F	17,156	16,715	14,998
M	17,087	16,649	14,930
A	17,144	16,733	14,980
M	17,124	16,633	14,954
J	17,108	16,621	14,929
J	17,214	16,705	15,009
A	17,289	16,764	15,055
S	17,457	16,817	15,193
O	17,566	16,877	15,276
N	17,636	16,866	15,320
D	17,605	16,904	15,268

	Total* Reserves	Required* Reserves	Reserves Avail. for Pvt. D.D.
1961			
J	17,701	16,986	15,325
F	17,748	17,108	15,312
M	17,734	17,163	15,270
A	17,909	17,304	15,421
M	17,864	17,293	15,340
J	17,993	17,358	15,445
J	17,961	17,361	15,381
A	18,010	17,421	15,403
S	18,077	17,492	15,446
O	18,140	17,599	15,479
N	18,320	17,701	15,637
D	18,248	17,765	15,558
1962			
J	18,428	17,841	15,678
F	18,228	17,741	15,407
M	18,339	17,844	15,467
A	18,483	17,988	15,575
M	18,443	17,923	15,510
J	18,439	17,946	15,472
J	18,498	17,964	15,496
A	18,446	17,899	15,422
S	18,370	17,911	15,316
O	18,561	18,048	15,463
N	18,744	18,159	15,602
D	18,778	18,253	15,596

	Total* Reserves	Required* Reserves	Reserves Avail. for Pvt. D.D.
1963			
J	18,882	18,426	15,629
F	18,862	18,405	15,553
M	18,888	18,437	15,538
A	19,019	18,601	15,643
M	19,042	18,561	15,634
J	18,981	18,582	15,551
J	19,163	18,682	15,710
A	19,089	18,640	15,581
S	19,141	18,728	15,603
O	19,284	18,839	15,692
N	19,466	19,034	15,795
D	19,528	19,053	15,818

REQUIRED RESERVES
6-Month Moving Average (Annual Rate)

1958		1959		1960		1961		1962		1963	
J	-.9	J	2.8	J	-5.0	J	3.4	J	5.5	J	5.1
F	.8	F	1.8	F	-4.2	F	4.1	F	3.7	F	5.6
M	1.4	M	2.9	M	-4.3	M	4.1	M	4.0	M	5.8
A	4.2	A	3.5	A	-2.6	A	5.0	A	4.4	A	6.1
M	5.3	M	3.0	M	-3.8	M	5.3	M	2.5	M	4.4
J	5.9	J	1.9	J	-2.8	J	4.4	J	2.1	J	3.6
J	8.0	J	2.9	J	-.8	J	3.7	J	1.4	J	2.8
A	7.3	A	1.1	A	.6	A	3.8	A	1.8	A	2.5
S	6.8	S	-.6	S	2.0	S	3.1	S	.8	S	3.1
O	4.6	O	-2.0	O	1.7	O	3.4	O	.7	O	2.3
N	4.4	N	-2.3	N	2.8	N	4.7	N	2.6	N	5.0
D	2.6	D	-2.9	D	3.4	D	4.7	D	3.4	D	5.0

Source: Fed. of St. Louis.
*Reserves of member banks less those behind treasury deposits.

193

CHART 3

RESERVE POSITION*
Monthly
(Millions of Dollars)

	1957 Excess	Borrowings	Free		1959 Excess	Borrowings	Free		1961 Excess	Borrowings	Free		1963 Excess	Borrowings	Free
J	523	407	+117	J	497	557	− 59	J	745	49	+696	J	483	99	+384
F	514	640	−126	F	460	508	− 47	F	654	137	+517	F	472	172	+300
M	518	834	−316	M	461	601	−140	M	546	70	+476	M	426	155	+271
A	506	1,011	−505	A	417	676	−258	A	618	56	+562	A	434	121	+313
M	465	909	−444	M	448	767	−318	M	549	96	+453	M	457	209	+248
J	496	1,005	−508	J	408	921	−513	J	612	63	+549	J	377	236	+141
J	534	917	−383	J	400	957	−557	J	581	51	+530	J	480	322	+158
A	534	1,005	−471	A	472	1,007	−535	A	604	67	+537	A	467	330	+137
S	522	988	−467	S	410	903	−493	S	584	37	+547	S	413	321	+ 92
O	467	811	−344	O	446	905	−459	O	507	65	+442	O	408	313	+ 95
N	512	804	−293	N	445	878	−433	N	622	105	+517	N	415	376	+ 39
D	577	710	−133	D	482	906	−424	D	568	149	+419	D	525	327	+198

	1958 Excess	Borrowings	Free		1960 Excess	Borrowings	Free		1962 Excess	Borrowings	Free
J	573	451	+122	J	544	905	−361	J	616	70	+546
F	567	242	+324	F	455	816	−361	F	502	68	+434
M	633	138	+495	M	416	635	−219	M	470	91	+379
A	623	130	+493	A	408	602	−194	A	510	69	+441
M	666	119	+547	M	469	502	− 33	M	497	63	+434
J	626	142	+484	J	466	425	+ 41	J	471	100	+371
J	656	109	+546	J	508	388	+120	J	532	89	+443
A	635	252	+383	A	540	293	+247	A	563	127	+436
S	571	476	+ 95	S	639	225	+414	S	458	80	+378
O	521	425	+ 96	O	638	149	+489	O	484	65	+419
N	506	486	+ 20	N	756	142	+614	N	592	119	+473
D	516	557	− 41	D	769	87	+682	D	572	304	+268

Source: Federal Reserve Bulletin, p. 3.
*All member banks; averages of daily figures since July, 1958.

CHART 7

DIFFUSION INDEXES

PERCENTAGE EXPANDING

1957	Leaders	Coincident	Laggers
J	25	92	99
F	8	88	71
M	13	81	92
A	38	71	100
M	42	58	88
J	46	75	79
J	25	75	88
A	21	58	77
S	4	13	75
O	0	8	58
N	17	17	58
D	21	21	58

1958	Leaders	Coincident	Laggers
J	21	0	29
F	25	21	21
M	50	25	21
A	75	67	13
M	75	71	0
J	100	88	0
J	92	92	29
A	100	88	21
S	100	88	67
O	79	100	67
N	83	100	79
D	79	100	79

1959	Leaders	Coincident	Laggers
J	83	100	88
F	79	100	79
M	100	100	88
A	92	96	79
M	67	100	79
J	25	81	88
J	17	17	100
A	17	17	71
S	25	21	79
O	29	71	71
N	62	81	100
D	71	79	83

1960	Leaders	Coincident	Laggers
J	71	81	67
F	33	69	71
M	17	81	79
A	17	58	88
M	33	79	88
J	25	21	71
J	25	38	42
A	25	38	42
S	29	46	42
O	21	29	50
N	17	4	58
D	25	21	50

1961	Leaders	Coincident	Laggers
J	29	21	40
F	58	50	0
M	92	69	21
A	92	81	30
M	75	81	30
J	54	88	50
J	71	94	60
A	67	81	80
S	83	94	90
O	71	94	69
N	79	94	69
D	54	88	69

1962	Leaders	Coincident	Laggers
J	58	81	69
F	62	94	90
M	50	94	90
A	54	94	100
M	17	75	80
J	17	94	90
J	0	75	60
A	25	69	60
S	62	75	50
O	79	81	70
N	75	75	50
D	54	69	70

1963	Leaders	Coincident	Laggers
J	62	62	50
F	62	75	50
M	71	75	70
A	67	75	90
M	71	94	80
J	38	100	90
J	29	100	80
A	54	75	70
S	88	75	90
O	71	69	70
N	62	88	70
D	54	88	60

Source: Statistical Indicator Associates.

195

CHART 10

COMPOSITE INDEX
(July, 1954 = 100)

1957	Leaders	Coincident	Laggers
J	122	120	125
F	118	120	125
M	117	122	126
A	113	122	126
M	115	121	127
J	118	121	127
J	116	122	129
A	111	122	129
S	107	120	130
O	103	119	130
N	101	117	130
D	100	117	129

1958	Leaders	Coincident	Laggers
J	96	115	128
F	95	111	126
M	95	111	125
A	93	110	123
M	99	110	121
J	100	112	120
J	104	112	119
A	109	113	119
S	110	114	119
O	116	116	119
N	117	117	120
D	117	118	121

1959	Leaders	Coincident	Laggers
J	119	119	121
F	123	120	122
M	127	122	123
A	131	125	125
M	130	126	127
J	127	126	128
J	126	126	130
A	122	124	131
S	122	124	133
O	121	124	134
N	118	124	135
D	128	126	135

1960	Leaders	Coincident	Laggers
J	126	127	137
F	123	128	136
M	117	127	136
A	119	129	136
M	119	128	135
J	115	128	135
J	114	127	136
A	115	127	136
S	113	127	137
O	114	126	138
N	112	125	138
D	108	124	138

1961	Leaders	Coincident	Laggers
J	111	124	136
F	111	123	137
M	118	124	138
A	121	125	139
M	122	126	139
J	120	126	139
J	125	127	139
A	122	128	138
S	128	128	138
O	128	130	138
N	128	132	138
D	128	132	138

1962	Leaders	Coincident	Laggers
J	127	133	139
F	128	133	140
M	134	135	140
A	131	136	142
M	130	136	142
J	122	136	143
J	120	137	143
A	120	136	144
S	120	137	145
O	124	138	145
N	125	138	145
D	126	139	146

1963	Leaders	Coincident	Laggers
J	126	140	146
F	129	139	146
M	129	140	147
A	132	141	148
M	133	140	149
J	136	142	150
J	131	144	151
A	133	143	152
S	135	144	152
O	140	145	153
N	131	144	154
D	135	146	154

Source: Statistical Indicator Associates.

CHART 11

GNP VELOCITY (All Commercial Banks)
(1956 = 100)

Year	GNP Velocity	(3.08) GNP Velocity Index
1909		
1910		
1911		
1912		
1913		
1914		
1915	3.27	106.2
1916	3.38	109.7
1917	3.66	118.8
1918	4.21	136.7
1919	3.97	128.9
1920	3.95	128.3
1921	3.35	108.8
1922	3.49	113.3
1923	3.82	124.0
1924	3.67	119.1
1925	3.71	120.5
1926	3.82	124.0
1927	3.74	121.4
1928	3.80	123.4
1929	4.00	129.9
1930	3.64	118.2
1931	3.27	106.2
1932	2.88	93.5
1933	2.92	94.8
1934	3.02	98.1
1935	2.84	92.2
1936	2.83	91.9
1937	3.00	97.4
1938	2.84	92.2

Year/Qtr	GNP Velocity	(3.08) GNP Velocity Index
1939		
I	2.80	90.9
II	2.74	89.0
III	2.70	87.7
IV	2.61	84.7
1940		
I	2.62	85.1
II	2.59	84.1
III	2.57	83.4
IV	2.55	82.8
1941		
I	2.58	83.8
II	2.72	88.3
III	2.76	89.6
IV	2.91	94.5
1942		
I	2.83	91.9
II	2.91	94.5
III	2.89	93.8
IV	2.90	94.2
1943		
I	2.73	88.6
II	2.73	88.6
III	2.58	83.8
IV	2.63	85.4
1944		
I	2.59	84.1
II	2.51	81.5
III	2.48	80.5
IV	2.37	77.0
1945		
I	2.32	75.3
II	2.28	74.0
III	2.11	68.5
IV	1.92	62.3

Year/Qtr	GNP Velocity	(3.08) GNP Velocity Index
1946		
I	1.93	62.7
II	1.95	63.3
III	2.02	65.6
IV	2.05	66.6
1947		
I	2.06	66.9
II	2.06	66.9
III	2.09	67.9
IV	2.17	70.5
1948		
I	2.21	71.8
II	2.30	74.7
III	2.35	76.3
IV	2.38	77.3
1949		
I	2.34	76.0
II	2.30	74.7
III	2.33	75.7
IV	2.32	75.3
1950		
I	2.37	77.0
II	2.41	78.3
III	2.55	82.8
IV	2.62	85.1
1951		
I	2.71	88.0
II	2.76	89.6
III	2.79	90.6
IV	2.78	90.3
1952		
I	2.76	89.6
II	2.74	89.0
III	2.74	89.0
IV	2.82	91.6

Year/Qtr	GNP Velocity	(3.08) GNP Velocity Index
1953		
I	2.86	92.9
II	2.87	93.2
III	2.85	92.5
IV	2.80	90.9
1954		
I	2.79	90.6
II	2.77	89.9
III	2.77	89.9
IV	2.81	91.2
1955		
I	2.88	93.5
II	2.93	95.1
III	2.99	97.1
IV	3.03	98.4
1956		
I	3.03	98.4
II	3.05	99.0
III	3.10	100.7
IV	3.15	102.3
1957		
I	3.20	103.9
II	3.23	104.9
III	3.27	106.2
IV	3.25	105.5
1958		
I	3.17	102.9
II	3.19	103.6
III	3.22	104.6
IV	3.27	106.2
1959		
I	3.32	107.8
II	3.41	110.7
III	3.36	109.1
IV	3.43	111.4

Year/Qtr	GNP Velocity	(3.08) GNP Velocity Index
1960		
I	3.54	114.9
II	3.59	116.6
III	3.58	116.2
IV	3.56	115.6
1961		
I	3.53	114.6
II	3.59	116.6
III	3.65	118.5
IV	3.71	120.5
1962		
I	3.76	122.1
II	3.79	123.1
III	3.83	124.4
IV	3.84	124.7
1963		
I	3.85	125.0
II	3.88	126.0
III	3.91	126.9
IV	3.93	127.6
1964		
I		
II		
III		
IV		
1965		
I		
II		
III		
IV		
1966		
I		
II		
III		
IV		

CHART 11
BUSINESS CYCLES

PEAK		TROUGH	
JAN.	1920	JUL.	1921
MAY	1923	JUL.	1924
OCT.	1926	NOV.	1927
JUN.	1929	MAR.	1933
MAY	1937	JUN.	1938
NOV.	1948	OCT.	1949
NOV.	1953	AUG.	1954
JUL.	1957	APR.	1958
MAY	1960	FEB.	1961

Index

199

This book has been set on the Linotype in 12 point Bodoni Book, leaded 2 points, and 10 point Bodoni Book, leaded 1 point. Chapter numbers and titles are in 18 point Bodoni Bold. The size of the type page is 24 by 42 picas.